Contents

CW00401843

Contents

Welcome

Welcome!

Welcome to **PagePlus X8**, the award-winning Desktop Publishing (DTP) solution from Serif. PagePlus is the easiest way to get superior publishing results, whether on your desktop or via professional printing. It's simple for anyone to create, publish and share their designs as outstanding printed documents, stunning PDFs, PDF slideshows, tables/charts, modern eBooks or via web page.

To make life so much easier, PagePlus comes with an impressive selection of design templates, creative content, and styles for you to use. As a result, publishing to a professional standard is easily achievable for experienced and inexperienced users alike! You'll also be able to reuse existing content by importing PDF documents and word processing documents. On the flipside, you'll be able to export drawn objects to all the latest graphic file formats.

PagePlus X8 doesn't stop at superior publishing. Its range of design studios makes PagePlus stand out from the crowd—**Cutout Studio** for cutting pictures out from their backgrounds, **LogoStudio** for custom logo design, and **PhotoLab** for powerful image adjustment and effect combinations. You simply cannot afford to miss them!

Registration

Don't forget to register your new copy, using the **Registration Wizard**, on the **Help** menu. That way, we can keep you informed of new developments and future upgrades!

New features

New features and enhancements introduced in PagePlus X8 give you more professional-looking publications, more control, more style, more design power, and new publishing capabilities!

Professional Text Handling

- **Text alignment to a Baseline Grid** (see p. 63)
  Give newsletters, brochures, magazines, programmes, handouts and other multi-column publications a clean, consistent, professional finish by neatly aligning text across different columns, frames, and pages, even when font sizes vary. Baseline Grid is available as a setting for entire publications or individual frames.

- **New text frame layout controls** (see p. 60)
  Give text in frames a neater look with column rules and fine tune spacing, or padding. Apply a mirrored layout for facing pages publications (that have different left and right pages). Uneven columns and margins can simply switch from one side of the frame to the other when moving between pages, without you having to edit text or frame settings.

- **Auto-Correct enhancements**
  Improvements include multi-word auto-correct, which can help insert phrases when you start a sentence, and automatic detection of lists, hyperlinks, and email addresses.

Digital Publishing and Design

- **Place PDFs**
  In addition to full PDF editing it's now also possible to simply place supplied PDFs into your publications and designs as non-editable

images, with an even higher level of import accuracy. Crop to trim boxes, bleed boxes, and more.

- **Improved EPUB digital publishing** (see p. 156)
  Take advantage of the power available to readers, computers, tablets and other displays by publishing with new EPUB 3 compatibility. Produce attractive designs with full layout, so publications like textbooks, comics, info sheets, children's books and sales sheets look just as you want when displayed on modern gadgets. Also benefit from new device-specific blank ePublications, themed templates, plus other EPUB improvements including publishing profiles, image size limits, and setting the first page as a cover.

- **New and improved filter effects** (see p. 115)
  Add a new Trail effect, add ripple effects to reflections, apply a cut off setting for feathering, a directional/gradient feather, and an outline and contoured line texture for variable-intensity drop shadows. Also now select from CMYK and scheme colours when formatting shadows, glows and other effects, ideal for high quality professional printing, single-colour print runs, or colour-scheming publications.

- **Document intent** (see p. 28)
  Choose from the outset whether you want your publication to conform to highly accurate print and PDF standards or to more closely match eReader and Web browser text rendering, and choose between CMYK or RGB colour modes. You can still publish in any format, but choosing the intent and colour space on set up gives you more accurate design and output.

- **Fresh theme layout and Pro templates**
  New Geo, Level, and Partition theme layouts provide sets of matching publications that can be adapted for a broad range of industries, clubs, charities and other end uses. New polished Pro template packs similarly offer a range of publications, a way to look highly contemporary and professional. Publications available to

each theme include letterheads and stationery, marketing materials, labels, and ePublications.

Advanced Control

- **Style your tables and calendars** (see p. 87)
  Improved table and calendar styles can be applied from an attractive gallery that pops down from the context toolbar. The Table AutoFormat designer gets a little makeover too, so it's easier to create and save your own table and calendar formats. Also access those custom styles from the new gallery.

- **Place objects with greater flexibility**
  Placement operations have been improved to include Place by Centre, Place by Diameter and Place by Radius. When placing multiple pictures (by importing files, scanning multiple photos, or opening multi-page publications) you can select and place pictures in the order you choose using a new pop-up window.

- **New hyperlink styling options**
  Hyperlinks are easier to style with publication-wide settings now incorporated into publication settings, and the ability to override settings for each hyperlink.

- **New fill and transparency controls**
  Easily edit fills and transparencies within updated, advanced Fill and Transparency editors, and access these new controls from other attribute dialogs, e.g. Character and Text Style settings.

Workspace

- **High DPI support**
  Windows display scaling is supported with automatic selection of suitably sized, sharp-looking buttons, controls and menus, so for very high-resolution displays, displays at a distance, or for those with impaired vision, PagePlus X8 will look better than ever.

- **Paragraph tab**
  Change paragraph settings without having to open a dialog—the new **Paragraph tab** adds popular controls to your tabbed workspace for greater efficiency.

Colours

- **Replace colours and manage the publication palette** (see p. 127)
  Replace regular colours across entire publications in one go, as easily as when updating colour schemes—ideal for quickly refreshing imported PDFs that do not use scheme colours. Manage your palette with new Clean and Update options, keeping it useful and tidy as designs evolve.

- **Colour picking from pictures**
  Load a picture directly into your Colour tab to grab colours without having to place on your page, so you can maintain focus on your design while picking co-ordinated colours.

- **Colour tab saturation control**
  A new slider on the Colour tab adjusts saturation, making it possible to easily select pastels, greys, and complementary tones.

- **New Pantone® colour palettes**
  Stay fashionable, design with a competitive edge, and print with confidence by choosing from 84 new, professionally-selected colours from an updated Pantone® PLUS palette.

Pictures

- **New photo editing tools and effects** (see p. 110)
  Vibrance, Split Tone, Tilt Shift, and Clarity PhotoLab filters add
  fantastic effects to enhance pictures, plus new tools offer selective
  editing and photo repair. Now control vignette positioning and
  sizing. Blend effects smoothly across an area using gradient masks,
  and remove unwanted blemishes, clutter or imperfections with a
  clone brush. Edit photos in your favourite program by launching
  any installed photo editor from PagePlus X8's context toolbar.

- **New scanning power**
  As manufacturers have been very slow to introduce 64-bit scanning
  software, PagePlus has been updated to support 32-bit and any
  newer 64-bit drivers, for both WIA and TWAIN driver types. Also
  scan and place multiple images in one operation if your scanner
  allows, without lifting the lid each time to swap pictures.

Installation

Installing PagePlus follows different procedures depending on whether
you are installing from disc or via download.

 You can install your new version alongside previous versions and
use them independently.

 32 or 64-bit PagePlus X8 installs to respective 32 or 64-bit
computers.

Installation procedure (from disc)

- Insert your purchased disc into your disc drive.

  - If AutoPlay is enabled on the drive, this automatically starts the Setup Wizard. Follow the on-screen instructions for install.

    -or-

  - If AutoPlay is not enabled (or doesn't start the install automatically), navigate to your program disc and double-click **autorun.exe**.

Installation procedure (from download)

- From serif.com, when logged into your Serif account, follow the on-screen instructions to download.

System Requirements

Minimum:

- Windows-based PC* with DVD drive and mouse

- Operating systems:
  Microsoft Windows® XP SP3 (32 bit)
  Windows® Vista (32 or 64 bit)
  Windows® 7 (32 or 64 bit)
  Windows® 8 (32 or 64 bit)

- 512MB RAM (Windows® XP)
  1GB RAM (Windows® Vista and 32-bit Windows 7® and 8)
  2GB RAM (For 64-bit Windows® 7 and 8)

- 510MB free hard disk space

- 1024 x 768 monitor resolution (at 100% scaling)
  1280 x 960 monitor resolution (at 125% scaling)
  1536 x 1152 monitor resolution (at 150% scaling)
  2048 x 1536 monitor resolution (at 200% scaling)

* Main processor must support SSE2 instructions.

Additional disk resources and memory are required when editing large and/or complex publications.

Recommended

As above but:

- Dual-core processor technology

- 1.8GB free hard disk space

Optional:

- Windows-compatible printer

- TWAIN-compatible scanner and/or digital camera

- .NET 2.0 for text import filters (Word 2007/2010 + OpenOffice) (installed by default)*

- Internet account and connection required for accessing online resources

* On Windows 8, also requires an extra 1GB of free hard disk space.

Getting Started

2

Startup Assistant

Once PagePlus has been installed, you're ready to start.

- For Windows Vista/7: Setup adds a **Serif PagePlus X8** item to the **All Programs** submenu of the Windows **Start** menu. Use the Windows **Start** button to pop up the Start menu, click on **All Programs** and then click **Serif PagePlus X8**.

- For Windows 8: The Setup routine during install adds a **Serif PagePlus X8** entry to the desktop. Use the Windows **Start** button to pop up the desktop, and then click the PagePlus icon.

On program launch, the Startup Assistant is displayed which offers different routes into PagePlus:

The options are described as follows:

-  The default home page keeps you in touch with Serif promotions and showcases articles (tutorials, etc.) You can also view the PagePlus Overview and Quick Start video

- **Open** - to access PagePlus publications, PDF files, or BookPlus files; also provides recent file history.

- **Learn** - for online video/written tutorials, help, tips & tricks, and more—all via a learn feed that can be filtered by article Type. The Product Help and your PagePlus X8 user guide are also provided.

- **New Publication** - creates a new publication from scratch, based on a choice of page setups.

- **Templates** - creates a new publication based on one of many design templates.

- **News** - for cross-product news, company news, articles, and product announcements, using Serif's news feed.

Any time you access the Startup Assistant, the Learn or News buttons indicate the number of new articles to be viewed (if available). This number will decrease as you read each article in the Learn or News pane.

When new articles arrive, these will be indicated the next time you open the Startup Assistant.

 Any new unread article arriving in the Learn or News pane will display a "new" indicator in its thumbnail.

Once you've clicked on a new article the "new" indicator changes to a "read" indicator.

Don't forget to use the keyword Search box at the top-right of the Startup Assistant. This is an incredibly powerful tool for filtering specific publication names, Learn articles, page sizes, theme layout names, or news articles.

Creating a publication from a design template

PagePlus comes complete with a whole range of categorized design templates which will speed you through the creation of all kinds of publications for desktop or commercial printing!

Each template offers:

- **Complementary design**—Professionally designed layout with high-visual impact.

- **Schemes**—choose a named colour scheme to apply a specific look and feel.

Design templates come in two types—**Theme Layouts**, where you pick your own pictures, or ready-to-go **Pro Templates** which are already populated with pictures.

Theme layouts offer a choice of themes (e.g., Ribbon) on which to base your publication (Brochure, Business Card, Flyer, Forms, Letterheads, Newsletter, ePublication, etc.); you'll get picture placeholders instead of actual pictures. Simply add your own pictures to placeholders and personalize placeholder text, then publish.

You can also choose which page layouts you want to base your new publication on.

Ready-to-go Pro templates
These are categorized templates containing royalty-free photos which can be adopted to fast-track you to your completed publication. You just need to personalize placeholder text, then publish.

To create a publication from a design template:

1. Open PagePlus, or select **Startup Assistant** from the **File** menu.

2. Click **Templates**.

3. From the pane, select a Theme Layout or a design template from the Pro Template Packs category. Select from the tree menu in the left-hand pane.
   - or -

   Scroll down to choose a publication type from the same list, e.g. Brochures, Business Cards, ePublications, etc.

4. Navigate the main window's categories and sub-categories using the ⊙ and ⊙ buttons to expand and collapse, then click your chosen thumbnail.

5. Examine the page sample(s) on the right. For theme layouts with multiple pages (e.g., brochures), you can choose which pages you wish to be part of your publication by checking the check box under each page. For design templates, simply review the pages to be part of your publication.

Theme Layouts   *Pro Design Templates*

6. Pick a colour scheme from the drop-down list at the top of the dialog. The page thumbnails refresh to reflect the new page's appearance.

7. Click **OK**. The pages are added to your new publication.

Starting a new publication from scratch

Although design templates can simplify your design choices, you can just as easily start out from scratch with a new, blank publication.

Page sizes are available for a range of publications including business cards, labels, and posters, with support for folded and ePublication publication setup.

To start a new publication (via Startup Assistant):

1. Open PagePlus to display the **Startup Assistant**.
    - or -
    Select **Startup Assistant** from the **File** menu (during your session).

2. Select **New Publication**.

3. From the main pane, navigate the document categories by scrolling (click the ⊙ icon to collapse categories if needed).

4. Click a thumbnail to create your new blank publication.

To create a publication using the default page type:

*   During your PagePlus session, click ⬚ **New Publication** on the **Standard** toolbar.

To create a custom publication:

1. From the Startup Assistant's New Publication pane, click **Custom Publication**.

2. From the Publication Setup dialog, select a publication type, size, and orientation.

3. Click **OK**.

> Choosing an **Intent** from **File>Publication Setup** which will help
> PagePlus more accurately represent how your publication will look
> when published or printed. Choose between the two **Print/PDF** and
> **eBook/Web** output types, preferably before you start creating
> content. You can also choose a colour mode (RGB or CMYK) that
> suits either on-screen viewing or printed output, respectively.

Opening existing publications

You can open a PagePlus publication from the **Startup Assistant**, **Standard** toolbar, or via the **File** menu.

It is also possible to open PDF files as new publications, or Import PDF files and existing PagePlus files into currently open publications. (See PagePlus Help for these import options.)

To open an existing publication (via Startup Assistant):

1. Open PagePlus to display the initial Startup Assistant.
   - or -
   Select **Startup Assistant** from the **File** menu (during your session).

2. Select **Open**.

3. Several options are possible:

   i. For recently opened publications, select a thumbnail from the main pane.

   ii. The publication opens in your workspace.

   - or -

iii.   For other PagePlus publications, PDF files, or BookPlus files, select from the Browse My Computer pane.

iv.   From the dialog, locate and select your file, then click **Open**.

To open existing publications (without Startup Assistant):

Click 📂 **Open** on the **Standard** toolbar.

Object management overview

Action	Tool/button/ command name	Toolbar/ Tab/key
Aligning	Align Objects	**Arrange** toolbar
	Align Top	**Align** tab
	Align Bottom	
	Align Left	
	Align Right	
	Horizontal Centre	
	Vertical Centre	
Combining	Convert to>Curves then Combine Curves	**Tools** menu then **Arrange** menu
Copying	Copy	**Standard** toolbar
Cropping	Square Crop Tool	**Attributes** toolbar
Cutting	Cut	**Standard** toolbar

Deleting		**Delete** Key
Distributing	Space Evenly Across Space Evenly Down	**Align** tab
Duplicating	-	-
Flip (horizontally)	Flip horizontal	**Arrange** menu
Flip (vertically)	Flip vertical	**Arrange** menu
Grouping	Group/ Ungroup	Under selected objects
Joining	Join Outlines	**Arrange** toolbar
Locking/ Unlocking	-	**Arrange** menu> Lock Objects **Arrange** menu> Unlock Objects
Moving	Pointer Tool	**Tools** toolbar
Ordering	Bring to Front Send to Back Forward One Back One	**Arrange** toolbar
Pasting	Paste	**Standard** toolbar

Placing	Place Multiple	**Context** toolbar
Selecting	Pointer Tool Lasso Tool	**Tools** toolbar
Replicating	-	**Edit** menu
Resizing	Pointer Tool	**Tools** toolbar
Rotating	Pointer Tool	**Tools** toolbar
	Rotate Left Rotate Right	**Arrange** toolbar

Updating and saving defaults

Object defaults are the stored property settings PagePlus applies to newly created objects such as:

- **lines** and **shapes** (line and fill colour, shade, pattern, transparency, etc.)

- **frames** (margins, columns, etc.)

- **text** (i.e., font, size, colour, alignment, etc.). Defaults are saved separately for **artistic, shape**, **frame** and **table text.**

You can easily change the defaults for any type of object via the **Update Object Default** command or the **Text Style Palette** dialog.

Default settings are always **local**—that is, any changed defaults apply to the current publication and are automatically saved with it, so they're in effect next time you open that publication. However, at any time you can use the **Save Defaults** command to record the current defaults as **global** settings that will be in effect for any new publication you subsequently create.

To set local defaults for a particular type of object:

1. Create a single sample object and fine-tune its properties as desired—or use an existing object that already has the right properties. (For graphics, you can use a line, shape, or rectangle; all share the same set of defaults.)

2. Select the object that's the basis for the new defaults and from the **Format** menu, select **Update Object Default**.

Or, for line and fill colours, including line styles:

1. With no object selected, choose the required line and/or fill colours from the Colour or Swatches tab. Use the Line tab to set a default line weight, style, and corner shape.

2. Draw your object on the page, which will automatically adopt the newly defined default colours and styles.

To view and change default text properties:

1. From the **Format** menu, select **Text Style Palette**.

2. Double-click **Default Text**, then from the expanded list of text types, choose an option (e.g., Artistic Text).

3. Click **Modify** to view current settings for the selected text type.

4. Use the Text Style dialog to alter character, paragraph, or other properties.

To save all current defaults as global settings:

1. From the **Tools** menu, select **Save Default Settings**.

2. From the dialog, check options to update specific defaults globally:

- **Document and object defaults** - saves current document settings (page size, orientation) and object settings (context toolbar settings).

- **Text styles** - saves current text styles in the Text Style Palette.

- **Object styles** - saves user-defined styles from Styles tab.

Click **Save** to confirm that you want new publications to use the checked object's defaults globally.

Saving your publication

To save your work:

1. Click ▥ **Save** on the **Standard** toolbar.

2. To save under a different name, choose **Save As** from the **File** menu.

> Unsaved publications have an asterisk after their name in the PagePlus title bar, **Publications** toolbar, and **Window** menu.

Pages

3

Setting up a publication

A publication's **page size**, **orientation** and **intent** settings are fundamental to your layout, and are defined when the new publication is first created, either using a design template or as a new publication. Properly setting up your publication size and intent at the outset reduces the chance of encountering problems when publishing and printing.

To adjust size/orientation of the current publication:

1. Select **Publication Setup** from the Pages context toolbar.

2. Ensure the **Paper** menu option is selected. The other option, **Margins**, lets you define non-printable Margin, Row, Column, and Bleed Guides as design aids.

3. For a **Regular/Booklet Publication**, you can select a pre-defined paper size, printer-derived paper size, or enter custom values for page **Width** and **Height**, as well as setting the orientation (Portrait or Landscape). For booklets only, select a type from the **Booklet** drop-down list, which page to start on (left/right), and if you require **Facing pages** (including **Dual master pages**). PagePlus automatically performs **imposition**.

4. For other publication types, you can select: **Small Publications** (for example, business cards, labels, etc.), **Large Publications** (banners or posters), or **Folded Publications** (cards).

    •   For Small publications, enable **Paper** and choose a pre-defined option from the list, or for creating **Labels**, enable the radio button and pick an Avery label code which matches your labels.

    •   For Large and Folded publications, choose a pre-defined option from the list (use the preview).

5. Click **OK** to accept the new dimensions. The updated settings will be applied to the current publication.

Once you've set up your publication, you can optionally include repeated page elements on every page by creating master pages (p. 33).

Intent

Setting the intent for your publication determines how text is composed and rendered, so should be decided at the start of your project.

> ⚠ Changing intent after you've finished designing can alter the appearance of your publication and can affect text flow. You may need to adjust text frame sizes and layouts.

1. In the **Publication Setup** dialog, click the **Intent** menu option.

2. Set the **Destination** to 'Print / PDF' or 'eBook / Web'.

   PagePlus composes text for Print/PDF output by default, so you should change it if publishing digitally as an eBook/web page, or designing for dual-purpose print and digital publishing.

3. Set the **Primary Colour Mode** to **RGB** or **CMYK**.

   This controls whether the publication uses a colour system that is most suitable for viewing on-screen (**RGB**) or for printing (**CMYK**) based on professional print inks.

   > 💡 If a preflight warning indicates an incorrect document intent, the offered 'fix' will automatically change the intent in this dialog to match the output to be published to.

   > 💡 If producing work professionally you may want to enable colour management. The publication's primary colour mode is also set in the **Colour Management** dialog.

Uniform and mixed page orientations

If you've changed your mind about the page orientation chosen at page setup, you can change the page orientation uniformly across your publication at any time.

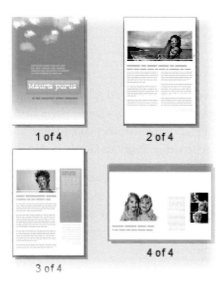

To change all publication pages from portrait to landscape (or vice versa):

- On the Pages context toolbar, click the down arrow on the **Publication Orientation** button, then select **Landscape Publication** (or **Portrait Publication**) from the flyout.

To change a page from portrait to landscape (or vice versa):

1. On the Pages tab, double-click to select a page.

2. Click **Change page orientation** to swap between portrait and landscape orientation.

- or -

From the Pages context toolbar, click the down arrow on the
Page orientation button, then select **Landscape Page** (or **Portrait Page**) from the flyout.

You can repeat the procedure for any other selected page.

Hyperlink colours

Hyperlink colours, on-page colour, background colour, and your background image can be set globally. Choose whether pages have individual background properties or whether they adopt publication settings. (See Setting page properties in PagePlus Help.)

By default, publications based on a template or those created from scratch use schemed colours for their hyperlink and on-page colours. These colours belong to the publication's current colour scheme but you can swap to a different scheme or change the individual colours at any time. See Using colour schemes on p. 128.

To set hyperlink, on-page and background colours:

1. Choose **Colours** from the **Publication Setup** dialog.

2. Click the down arrow for the hyperlink, on-page, or background colour you want to change.

3. Select a different colour from the flyout, which shows numbered scheme colours and other colours. Select **More Colour** to optionally pick from a **Colour Selector** dialog.

4. Click **OK**.

To remove underline style from hyperlink text:

1. From the **Publication Setup** dialog, choose the **Colours** menu option.

2. Uncheck **Underlined** adjacent to the relevant hyperlink colour.

To set a background image:

1. Choose **Colours** from the **Publication Setup** dialog and click **Background Image**.

2. In the **Background** dialog, check Use Background Image and pick an image:

3. Click **OK**.

> Background colours or images are not applied to pages on creation. To apply these publication settings, right-click the page, select **Page Properties** and check **Use publication settings**. (See Setting page properties in PagePlus Help.)

> Uncheck **Use Background Image** to disable the image background after use (but retaining the original image settings).

> If you use an image background with transparent regions, the Background colour is still active and will show through; otherwise the picture will cover the background colour.

Adding, removing, and rearranging pages

Use the **Pages tab** to add/delete standard or master pages, assign master pages to standard pages, and rearrange standard pages using drag-and-drop. You can also change page orientations.

To add a single page:

1. On the **Pages** tab, click once to select a page in the **Pages** window. The thumbnail that's shown as "selected" is independent of the page

you're currently working on. To work on a particular page, double-click its thumbnail.

2. Click ⬜ **Add** to add a page (or master page) *before* the one selected in the window.

    - or -

    To add a new page *at the end* of the publication, deselect all pages by clicking in the neutral region of the lower window, then click the **Add** button.

To add master pages:

For master pages, the above procedure applies but you need to click **Master Pages** to open its window first.

To delete a single page/master page:

1. On the **Pages** tab, select the page (or master page) to delete on the appropriate window by clicking its thumbnail.

2. Click ⬜ **Remove**.

To rearrange pages:

● On the **Pages** tab, in the lower **Pages** window, drag a page thumbnail over another page thumbnail in the page sequence. The page is added after the hovered over page thumbnail.

Adding more template pages

Use the Assets tab's Asset Browser if you're looking to use some additional template pages in your publication. See Browsing on p. 50.

You can drag-and-drop a page to replace (or add before/after) your current page.

Understanding master pages

Master pages provide a flexible way to store background elements that you'd like to appear on more than one page—for example a logo, background, header/footer, or border design.

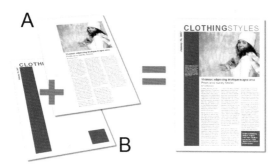

*(**A**) Page, (**B**) Master Page*

The key concept here is that a particular master page is typically **shared** by multiple pages, as illustrated below. By placing a design element on a master page and then assigning several pages to use that master page, you ensure that all the pages incorporate that element. Of course, each individual page can have its own "foreground" elements.

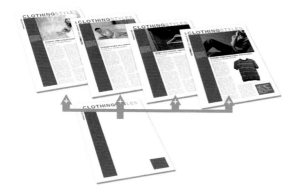

Master pages are available in every publication, but in a simple publication you may not need to use any master pages—or you may need only one master page. Facing pages and multiple master pages prove valuable with longer, more complex publications.

> If you're starting with a design template you may encounter one or more master pages incorporated with the design.

Using the **Pages** tab or **Page Manager**, you can quickly add or delete master pages; for example, you could set up different master pages for "title" or "chapter divider" pages.

Assigning master pages

If you're only using one master page it is assigned to any newly created page by default. However, if you're using multiple master pages you can assign a different master page to a standard page, all, odd or even pages. It's even possible to assign multiple master pages per page.

> You'll need to create an additional master page first. See Adding, removing, and rearranging pages on p. 31.

> Each new page or master page consists of a single layer; a page with a master page also shows the master page's Master Layer.

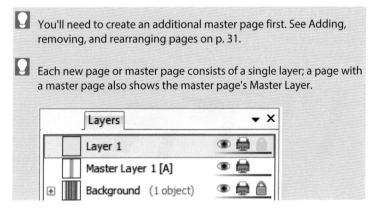

To assign a master page:

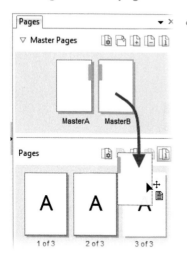

- From the expanded Master Pages window in the Pages tab, drag a master page onto a target standard page in the lower window.

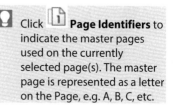

Click **Page Identifiers** to indicate the master pages used on the currently selected page(s). The master page is represented as a letter on the Page, e.g. A, B, C, etc.

Assigning multiple master pages

Just like a regular page, the master page can have its own set of layers associated with it, completely unique from the regular page! For a single master page assigned to a page, on the Layers tab, you'll see a master layer (e.g., 'Master Layer 1 [A]') as a separate entry. However, you can assign additional master pages to your page for more powerful page design.

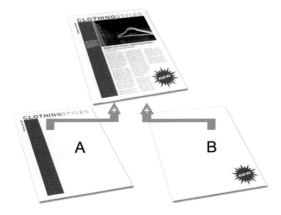

In the example above, a newly assigned master page B would add a new master layer ('Master Layer 2 [B]') to the publication page's Layers tab.

For an introduction to the concept of layers, see Working with layers on p. 42.

 An additional master page needs to be created first. See Adding, removing, and rearranging pages on p. 31.

To assign multiple master pages to a page:

- On the **Pages** tab, **Ctrl**-drag a master page thumbnail from the Master Page window onto the chosen page's thumbnail in the Pages window.

To jump to a master page from the selected publication page:

- Double-click on a Master Layer entry in the Layers tab.

The master page assigned to the master layer is displayed.

Facing pages and dual master pages

If you're using multi-page regular/booklet publications, you can assign different master pages to the left and right publication pages (also called spreads) if necessary—master pages are assigned per page and not per spread. For example (see below), a left-hand "body text" page might use the left-side component of one master page (**A**), while a right-hand page could use the right side of a different master page (**B**).

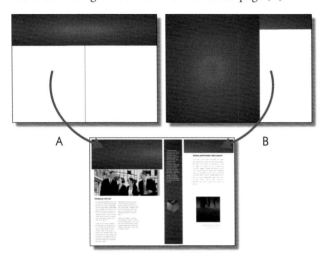

Editing master page objects

If you're editing pages which use master pages, master page objects will contribute to your page design. These objects can be edited quickly and easily from the page by using a control bar under the selected object.

- Click  **Edit on Master Page** to jump to the master page and edit the object there.

- Click ⌃A **Promote from Master Page** to disconnect the object from the master page and make it independently editable on the publication page.

Using page numbering

Page number fields automatically display the current page number. Typically, these fields are added automatically to the master page (so they appear on every page) with the Header and Footers Wizard (**Insert** menu), but you can insert a page number field anywhere in your master page text.

You can change the style of page numbers, create mixed page number formats, set starting page number(s), and control number continuation across chapters and publication sections (all via **Page Number Format** on the **Format** menu).

To insert a page number field:

1. Switch to the master page (if desired) by clicking ⧉1 **View Master Pages** on the Hintline.

2. With the **Artistic Text Tool** selected (**Tools** toolbar), click for an insertion point to place the page number.

3. On the **Insert** menu, select **Page Number** from the **Information** flyout.

You can also specify the **First Page Number** in the sequence (this will appear on the first page of the publication). For example, Chapter Two of a long publication might be in a separate file and begin numbering with page 33.

To set the first page number:

1. Uncheck **Continue from previous chapter**. PagePlus keeps this checked by default so that number continuation is maintained if your publication is to be part of a book.

2. Enter a different **First Page Number**.

For simple publications, it's likely that the same page format is used (e.g., Arabic numerals throughout). However, for more complex publications, different formats can be used for different page ranges, with each page range belonging to its own **publication section**. See PagePlus Help.

Navigating pages

To switch between pages:

*   On the **Pages** tab, double-click the page's thumbnail for the page (or master page) you want to view.

To switch between current page and its master page:

*   From the **Hintline**, click **Master Pages**.

Viewing pages

Most of the PagePlus display is taken up by a page or "artwork" area and a surrounding "pasteboard" area.

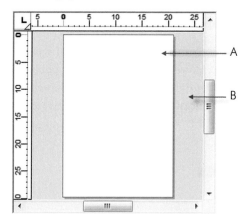

In PagePlus, the **Page** area (**A**) is where you add and position your text, shapes, and pictures that you want to print. The **Pasteboard** area (**B**) is where you generally keep any text, shapes, or pictures that are being prepared or waiting to be positioned on the page area.

To move or copy an object between pages via the Pasteboard:

1. Drag the object from the source page onto the pasteboard (hold down the **Ctrl** key to copy).

2. Use the page navigation buttons on the Hintline to jump to a target page.

3. Drag (or **Ctrl**-drag to copy) the object from the pasteboard onto the target page.

> In Multi-page view, you can simply drag the copy from one page to another.

PagePlus makes it easy to see exactly what you're working on—from a wide view of multiple pages to a close-up view of a small region. For example, you can use the **scroll bars** at the right and bottom of the main window to move the page and pasteboard with respect to the main window. If you're using a **wheel mouse**, you can scroll vertically by rotating the wheel, or horizontally by **Shift**-scrolling.

Magnifying pages

For magnification options, the **Hintline** toolbar provides the:

Zoom to Current option to zoom to a selected object, or to the page width if no objects are selected.

Zoom Tool to zoom into an area defined by a drawn marquee selection.

Pan Tool for moving around the zoomed-in page area by dragging.

Current Zoom option to display or change the level of magnification. To change, click to select from a flyout or enter a custom percentage value directly.

Zoom Out and **Zoom In** tools so you can inspect and/or edit the page at different levels of detail. Alternatively, use the Zoom slider to alter the zoom level instead these buttons.

The **Hintline** toolbar's **View Options** drop-down list also offers multi-page display/fitting options.

Working with layers

When you create a new publication from scratch or from some design templates, the page(s) you create will initially consist of two **layers**—one for the page (Layer 1) and one for the associated master page (see p. 33). The layers can be seen within a hierarchical stack on the **Layers tab**.

One layer may be enough to accommodate the elements of a particular layout, but you can create additional layers as needed for the page. However, multiple layers are useful when you're working on a complex design where it makes sense to separate one cluster of objects from another. You can work on one layer at a time without worrying about affecting elements on a different layer.

A useful feature of the Layers tab is that you can see objects under the layer on which they were created. By expanding the layer by clicking ⊞ , these objects are displayed—with a click, they can be selected on the page.

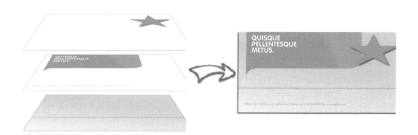

Master Layer, Layer 1 and Layer 2 from bottom to top.

Cumulative layers as seen on the page.

In order to create new objects on a particular layer, you'll need to select the layer.

To select a particular layer:

- Click a layer name. The layer entry then possesses a dark blue background.

To display master page layers:

- Double-click the master layer entry. The Layers tab now shows the master page's layers. The master page is now shown in the workspace.

For more information about master pages and assigning them to pages, see Understanding master pages on p. 33.

Adding, removing, and rearranging layers

Once you've created a page, it's easy to add, delete, or move layers as needed. Moving a layer by dragging will place its objects in the front or back of those on other layers.

To add a new layer to the current page or master page:

1. In the Layers tab, click ✛ **Add Layer**.

2. You'll be prompted to give the new layer a name and set its properties. When you've made your selections, click **OK**.

The new layer is inserted above the currently selected layer. If a layer is not selected, the new layer is placed at the top of the stack.

To delete a layer:

- In the Layers tab, select the layer's name and click ▭ **Delete Selected Layers**.

You can also move layers with associated objects. (See PagePlus Help for more details.)

Layer names and properties

The Layers tab lets you rename layers and set a variety of properties for one or more layers.

To rename the layer:

1. In the Layers tab, select the layer first, then click on its name.

2. At the insertion point, type a new name then either press the Return key or click away from the tab.

To set layer properties:

- Display the Layers tab.

    Select desired settings for the selected layer.

    - Click the **Make Invisible** icon to hide the layer and any objects on it; click again to reveal the layer.

    - Click the **Make Non-printable** icon to exclude the layer in page printouts; click again to include it.

    - Click the **Make Locked** icon to prevent objects on the layer from being selected/edited; click again to allow editing.

> You cannot select objects on a layer that is locked or not visible.

Double-click a layer or click **Layer Properties** to change selection handle colour and extend settings to layers with the same name. See Layers tab in PagePlus Help.

Assets for Creativity

4

Using assets

An **asset** is a general term for any object or page element that can be added to your page to enhance its appearance, increase efficiency, or personalize your design. Assets range from graphics, logos, pictures, picture frames, and backgrounds (as shown below), to more complex page content and entire pages.

To use assets, PagePlus provides the **Assets tab**, powered by both an Asset Browser (p. 50) and Asset Manager. The former browses your assets, the latter lets you create and manage custom Asset Packs.

 Theme Layout design templates come complete with their own built-in assets, all themed to the publication's design. When you start from a theme layout the Assets tab will be populated with associated assets automatically!

Using the Assets tab

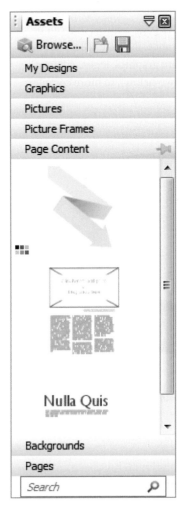

The Assets tab is a powerful design resource that exclusively hosts your browsed assets, ready for adding to your publication page.

Assets can be placed into the following categories.

- **My Designs**: Stores custom assets dragged from the page.

- **Graphics**: Stores professional clipart from Asset Packs.

- **Pictures**: Stores added pictures from your hard disk (or from Asset Pack, if containing pictures).

- **Picture Frames**: Stores picture frames from Asset Packs.

- **Page Content**: Stores page content (pre-assembled from various page objects) from Asset Packs.

- **Backgrounds**: Stores backgrounds from Asset Packs.

- **Pages**: Stores complete ready-to-go pages from Asset Packs.

The tab also lets you create custom designs for reuse globally or just in your publication. You'll be able to:

- Store your own designs to the tab's My Designs category for global use.

- Store your own designs to any other tab's category for current publication use.

- Create custom picture frames from drawn shapes.

- Create custom page backgrounds from pictures or filled page objects.

- Create custom page content (combinations of assets).

Although initially empty, the tab can be populated with assets of your choice by using an Asset Browser.

The Asset Browser

The Asset Browser lets you browse by asset category and Asset Pack (Pack Files), as well as search (by tag) for assets. Once displayed, the asset can be selected for inclusion in the Assets tab. See Browsing (p. 50) for more information.

The Asset Manager

Use the **Asset Manager** to create your own Asset Packs by using assets from other Asset Packs and/or by importing pictures, graphics, or backgrounds. You can tag assets and then save or export your custom asset pack. See Creating custom Asset Packs in PagePlus Help.

Browsing

The **Asset Browser** offers a whole range of professional ready-to-go designs that you can use directly in your publication. These designs are provided in categorized Asset Packs installed with PagePlus. You can browse these packs and preview their contents, before adding assets to your workspace.

There are two ways to browse assets—by category or by Asset Pack. You can also use the search controls at the top-right of the dialog to narrow your search, or to find a specific asset.

To browse assets (by category):

1. From the Assets tab, click **Browse**.

2. In the **Asset Browser**, select an asset category from the **Categories** section. You'll see installed Asset Packs appear in the main pane, stored under their Pack file names, e.g. Arctic.

3. Scroll through the asset packs to browse assets included in each pack.

To browse assets (by Asset Pack):

1. In the **Asset Browser**, on the left-hand side of the dialog, select an asset pack name from the **Pack Files** section, e.g., Backgrounds. The Asset Pack will appear in the main pane.

2. The assets are categorized further in the main pane by the name of the Asset Pack to which they belong, e.g., Fun. Scroll through to browse the assets included in each Asset Pack. To make browsing easier, you can expand and collapse the Asset Packs to hide or reveal the assets.

3. (Optional) To narrow your search, filter assets by entering an asset name in the **Search** box at the top-right of the main pane.

Searching for assets

The search facility filters assets based on preset and custom tags applied to all of the Asset Packs shown in the **Asset Browser**.

To apply a search filter:

- For a simple tag search, type the word or letter you want to search for in the **Search** text box, situated at the top right of the dialog. This is useful for retrieving assets with custom tags attached.

Filtering assets

Filtering means that you can restrict the amount of assets on display.

- For **category** and/or **pack file filtering**, select a category or pack file (or multiple instances using **Ctrl**-click). You can also search for category and pack file combinations. For example, selecting the Picture Frames category and then a Theme Layout gives you just picture frames from that theme layout.

- For **Smart tag filtering**, select a tag name from the **Smart Tags** section. Smart tags let you filter assets logically by subject matter using a hierarchical and alphabetic tag structure. For example, if you select the 'Food & Drink' tag you'll see all assets tagged with that tag; if you want food-only assets, you could select 'Food', nested under that Food & Drink tag.

- For **single-tag filtering**, select a tag name from the **Tags** section of the Asset Browser. (You may need to scroll down the left-hand pane to view). Use **Ctrl**-click to manually select multiple tags.

Adding assets to your Assets tab

To add a specific asset:

- Select the category or pack file in the Asset Browser, and then simply click the asset. A check mark shows on the thumbnail.

To add all assets:

- Click **Add All** 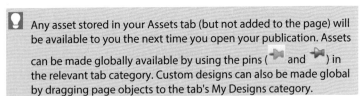 from the upper-right corner of each Asset Pack's thumbnail gallery. Check marks will show on all thumbnails.

With either method, asset(s) will be available to you from the Assets tab when you close the Asset Browser.

> Any asset stored in your Assets tab (but not added to the page) will be available to you the next time you open your publication. Assets can be made globally available by using the pins (and   ) in the relevant tab category. Custom designs can also be made global by dragging page objects to the tab's My Designs category.

Adding assets to your page

To add an asset to the page:

- Click an asset's thumbnail in your chosen category and drag it onto the page.

Text

5

Understanding text frames

Typically, text in PagePlus goes into **text frames**, which work equally
well as containers for single words, standalone paragraphs, multipage
articles, or chapter text.

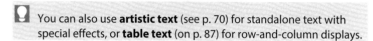

You can also use **artistic text** (see p. 70) for standalone text with
special effects, or **table text** (on p. 87) for row-and-column displays.

What's a text frame?

A text frame is a container (like a mini-page) in which the main text for
your publication is stored; in PagePlus, the text in the frame is actually
called a **story**.

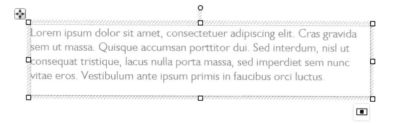

The text frame can be sized and positioned in advance of, or after,
adding body text. When you move a text frame, its **story text** moves
with it. When you resize a text frame, its story text reflows to the new
dimensions.

Perhaps the most important feature of text frames is the ability to flow
text between linked text frames on the same or different pages. See
Fitting text to frames on p. 65.

For now we'll look at a text frame as an object and the frame text
contained within a single frame.

Frame linking

Frames can be linked so that a single story continues from one frame to another. But text frames can just as easily stand alone. Thus in any publication, you can create text in a single frame, spread a story over several frames, and/or include completely independent frames. By placing text frames anywhere, in any order, you can build up newspaper or newsletter style publications with a story flowing:

- between linked frames on the same page.

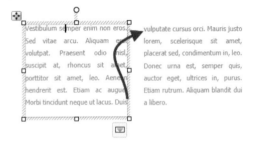

- between linked frames on different pages.

- from one column to another in the same frame.

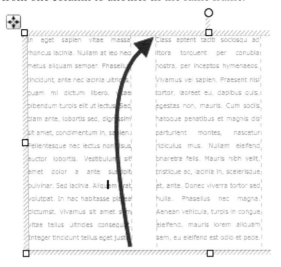

Creating text frames

You add text frames and position them on the page as you would any other object, in advance of adding text content.

To create a frame:

1. Select 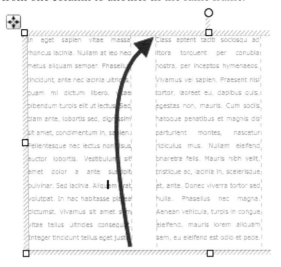 **Standard Text Frame** on the **Tools** toolbar.

2. Click on the page or pasteboard to create a new frame at a default size.
   - or -
   Drag out to place the text frame at your chosen dimensions.

To delete a frame:

- Select the frame—click its edge until a solid border appears—and then press the **Delete** key.

You can select, move, and resize text frames just like other objects (see PagePlus Help for details). When you select a frame's bounding box, indicated by a solid border, you can manage the frame properties; selecting inside a frame creates a blinking insertion point in the frame's text (the frame's boundary box becomes hatched to indicate editing mode). In this mode, you can edit the text. (For details, see Editing text on the page on p. 72.)

Putting text into a frame

You can put text into a frame using one of the following methods:

WritePlus story editor:	With a selected frame, click $\boxed{A\underline{I}}$ **Edit story in WritePlus** on the Frame context toolbar.
Importing text:	Select the frame, then select **Text File** from the **Insert** menu.
Typing into the frame:	Select the Pointer Tool, then click for an insertion point to type text straight into a frame, or edit existing text. (See Editing text on the page on p. 72.)
Pasting via the Clipboard:	At an insertion point in the text, press **Ctrl+V**.
Drag and drop:	Select text (e.g. in a word processor file), then drag it onto the PagePlus page.

Adding pictures into a text frame

Pictures can be placed inline at any point in your story in a text frame, with PagePlus prompting you to resize the picture to fit with the text frames dimensions if it is too large.

If you add further story text before the picture, the inline picture will move with the surrounding text.

To add a picture to a text frame:

1. Add an empty paragraph to your text frame at the point you want to add your picture, i.e. press Return at the end of an existing paragraph.

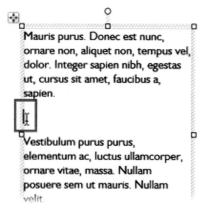

2. From the [image] ▼ **Picture** flyout on the **Tools** toolbar, click [image] **Import Picture**.

3. Navigate to your picture, select it and click **Open**.

4. If the picture dimensions exceed those of the text frame, click **Yes** in the displayed dialog to scale down the picture.

Frame properties and layout

The **frame layout** controls how text will flow in the frame. The frame can contain multiple **columns**. When a frame is selected, its column margins appear as dashed grey guide lines if set in **Frame Properties**. Note that unlike the page margin and row/column guides, which serve as layout guides for placing page elements, the frame column guides actually determine how text flows within each frame. Text won't flow outside the column margins.

You can drag the column guides or use a dialog to adjust the top and bottom **column blinds** and the left and right **column margins**.

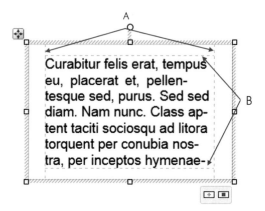

*(**A**) Column margins, (**B**) Column blinds.*

To edit frame properties directly:

* Select the frame object, then drag column guide lines to adjust the boundaries of the column.

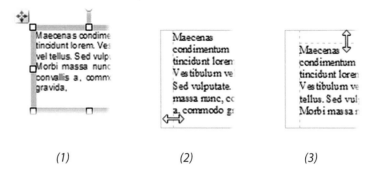

(1)	*(2)*	*(3)*

The frame edge is clicked to show a **selected** bounding box (**1**), after dragging inwards the column margin can be adjusted (**2**), and after dragging downwards, the top margin blind can be moved (**3**).

To edit frame properties using a dialog:

1. Select the frame and click 📄 **Text Frame Properties** on the Frame context toolbar.

2. From the dialog, use the three menu options to set up your frame.

   - **General**: precisely define frame padding and column margins (**Left** and **Right**), and enable/disable text wrapping around an object.

   - **Columns**: set the **Number of columns**, and, for each column set the column **Width**, Column Blinds (**Top**, **Bottom**), **Gutter** distance between columns, and if you want to apply column **Rules** between columns. To change any value, click a column cell in the table and enter a new value.

   - **Baseline grid**: enable a **Baseline grid** for your frame text. (See Baseline grid.)

3. Click **OK**.

To apply the same values across all columns in the dialog, hover over a column header, then select 'Make Values Equal', 'Set Values to Lowest', or 'Set Values to Highest' using the drop-down menu.

If you're using facing pages, PagePlus's Frame Setup lets you 'mirror' text frames appearing on left and right pages of a page spread with respect to frame settings (margins, columns etc.). Separate or linked text frames can be mirrored across the spread equally.

To mirror text frames:

1. In the **Frame Properties** dialog, check **Mirror settings for left and right pages**.

2. Copy and paste the text frame to the opposite page of the page spread. The new text frame will be a mirror of the original text frame.

Column rules can be created to help visually separate text in different columns. This is especially useful for multi-column text frames which contain large amounts of text. You can only add a column rule if you have set up two columns or more in your text frame.

Baseline grid

Clean and consistent typography is very important in design. PagePlus X8's baseline grid eases the process, using a global document alignment grid or grids for individual text frames. The grid is strictly for text alignment and is non-printing, so you only see it while designing.

When to use a Baseline Grid

The baseline grid layout option should be enabled when you want the neatest text layout, especially when composing using multi-column text frames or multiple frames per page. The baseline grid is a finishing process during text composition, applied after character size, line spacing and paragraph spacing considerations.

Applying a baseline grid setting to individual text frames overrides a publication's baseline grid, but for consistency it's recommended that you use a publication baseline grid.

Adding baseline grids

To add a baseline grid:

1. From the Pages context toolbar, select ▣ **Options**.

2. In the left of the window, select the **Baseline Grid** option in the **Layout** section.

3. Check the **Baseline Grid** setting and adjust start point, spacing, and display options if required.

⚠️ Text will not align to a baseline grid unless its paragraph properties have the **Align to Baseline Grid** setting enabled; this is enabled by default on new frame text. This is only available to text frames and paragraphs within text frames, it cannot be applied to artistic text.

Adding a baseline grid to an individual text frame

Any text frame can have its own baseline grid that is independent of a
publication-wide grid. While for neatest layouts a publication-wide grid
is recommended, applying a grid to an individual text frame gives you
more control.

To apply a baseline grid to an individual text frame:

1. Select a text frame you want to apply the baseline grid to.

2. From the Frame context toolbar, select [image] **Frame Properties**.

3. Select **Baseline Grid** in the left of the window.

4. Check the **Baseline Grid** setting and adjust start point, spacing, and
   the display option as required.

5. Click **OK**.

> If you can't see your baseline grid immediately, check your
> magnification level (by default the grid will not show below a zoom
> level of 70%), that **View>Grids and Guides>Baseline Grid** is
> checked, and that Clean Design is switched off.

Snapping to baseline grid

Once your baseline grid is added and text neatly aligns to the grid, it's
also possible to have other objects (shapes, pictures, etc.) make use of the
baseline grid for perfect alignment with text frames.

To snap to a baseline grid:

- From the **View** menu, select **Grids and Guides>Snap to Baseline
  Grid**.

Fitting text to frames

Fitting story text precisely into a sequence of frames is part of the art of laying out publications.

If there's too much story text to fit in a frame sequence, PagePlus stores it in an invisible **overflow area** and the Link button on the last frame of the sequence displays ▣; an ⊕ **AutoFlow** button appears next to the Link button. You might edit the story down or make more room for it by adding an extra frame or two to the sequence. Clicking the AutoFlow button adds additional frames and pages as needed (see below).

Once frames are in position it's still possible to control how text is distributed throughout the frame(s) via the Frame context toolbar.

 The **Text Sizing** flyout offers tools for controlling how frame text scales through the text frame. These are "one-off" operations (compared to the **Autofit** options shown below).

 Fit Text
Click to scale the story's text size so it fits exactly into the available frame(s); further text added to the frame will cause text overflow. You can use this early on, to gauge how the story fits, or near the end, to apply the finishing touch. Fit Text first applies small point size changes, then small leading changes, then adjustments to the paragraph space below value, until the text fits.

 Enlarge Text
Click to increase the story's text size one increment (approx. 2%).

 Shrink Text
Click to reduce the story's text size one increment (approx. 2%).

Each frame's story text can adopt its own individual autofit setting:

 The **AutoFit Options** flyout offers three autofit options which continuously act upon a selected frame's story text.

No AutoFit

This is the normal mode of operation where, if selected, text won't automatically scale throughout the selected text frame, possibly leaving partly empty frames at the end of the frame sequence.

Shrink Text on Overflow

If selected, extra text added to a selected frame will shrink all frame text to avoid text overflow.

AutoFit

If selected, the frame will always scale text automatically by adjusting text size (compare to **Fit Text** which fits text once, with any additional text causing text overflow).

AutoFlow

When importing text, it's a good idea to take advantage of the **AutoFlow** feature, which will automatically create text frames and pages until all the text has been imported. This way, enough frames are created to display the whole story. Then you can gauge just how much adjustment will be needed to fit the story to the available "real estate" in your publication.

If you add more text to a story while editing, or have reduced the size of a frame, you may find that an overflow condition crops up. In this case you can decide whether to use AutoFit or click the frame's **AutoFlow** button.

To AutoFlow story text on the page:

- Click the  **AutoFlow** button just to the left of the frame's 🔲 **Link** button.

If no other empty frames are detected, you'll be prompted to autoflow text into a new frame(s) the same size as the original or to new frame(s) sized to the page. If an empty frame exists anywhere in your publication, PagePlus will detect the first empty frame and prompt to flow text into this. At the dialogs, Click Yes to flow into frame or click No to let PagePlus detect and jump to the next empty frame.

Linking text frames

When a text frame is selected, the frame includes a **Link** button at the bottom right which denotes the state of the frame and its story text. It also allows you to control how the frame's story flows to following frames:

No Overflow
The frame is not linked to a following frame (it's either a standalone frame or the last frame in a sequence) and the frame is empty or the end of the story text is visible.

Overflow

The populated frame is not linked (either standalone or last frame) and there is additional story text in the **hidden** overflow area.

An 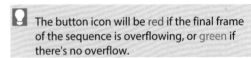 **Autoflow** button also appears to the left of the **Link** button.

Continued

The frame is linked to a following frame. The end of the story text may be visible, or it may flow into the following frame.

> The button icon will be red if the final frame of the sequence is overflowing, or green if there's no overflow.

There are two basic ways to set up a linked sequence of frames:

- You can link a sequence of empty frames, then import the text.

- You can import the text into a single frame, then create and link additional frames into which the text automatically flows.

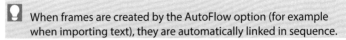

> When frames are created by the AutoFlow option (for example when importing text), they are automatically linked in sequence.

To create a link or reorder the links between existing frames, you can use the **Link** button under the frame. Remember to watch the cursor, which changes to indicate these operations.

- You can link to frames already containing text or are already in a link sequence.

- If the frame was not part of a link sequence, its text is merged into the selected text's story.

To link the selected frame to an existing frame:

1. Click the frame's **Link** button (showing or .)

2. Click with the Textflow cursor on the frame to be linked to.

To link the selected frame to a newly drawn frame:

- As above, but instead of clicking a "target" frame, either click on the page (for a default frame) or drag across the page (to create a frame sized to your requirements). The latter is ideal for quickly mapping out linked frames across different pages.

To unlink the selected frame from the sequence:

- Click on **Continued**, then click with the Textflow cursor on the same frame.

Story text remains with the "old" frames. For example, if you detach the second frame of a three-frame sequence, the story text remains in the first and third frames, which are now linked into a two-frame story. The detached frame is always empty.

Using artistic text

Artistic text is standalone text you type directly onto a page. Especially useful for headlines, pull quotes, and other special-purpose text, it's easily formatted with the standard text tools.

To create artistic text:

1. Choose the **A** **Artistic Text Tool** from the **Tools** toolbar.

2. Click on the page to make an insertion point from where you'll begin typing.

3. Set initial text properties (style, font, point size, etc.) using the Text context toolbar.

4. Start typing to create the artistic text using your chosen text properties.

Once you've created an artistic text object, you can select, move, resize, delete, and copy it just as you would with a text frame. Solid colours, gradient/bitmap fills, and transparency can all be applied.

To resize or reproportion an artistic text object:

- To resize while maintaining the object's proportions, drag the resize handles.

- To resize freely, hold down the **Shift** key while dragging.

To edit artistic text:

- Drag to select a range of text, creating a blue selection.

You can also double-click to select a word, or triple-click to select all text.

Now you can type new text, apply character and paragraph formatting, edit the text in WritePlus, apply proofing options, and so on.

Editing text on the page

You can use the Pointer Tool to edit frame text, table text, or artistic text directly. On the page, you can select and enter text, set paragraph indents and tab stops, change text properties, apply text styles, and use Find and Replace.

Selecting and entering text

The selection of frame text, artistic text, and table text follows the conventions of the most up-to-date word-processing tools. The selection area is shaded in semi-transparent blue for clear editing.

> Nulla vestibulum eleifend
> nulla. Suspendisse potenti.
> Aliquam turpis nisi, venenatis
> non, accum san nec, imperdiet
> laoreet, lacus.

Double-, triple- or quadruple-click selects a word, paragraph or all text, respectively. You can also make use of the **Ctrl**-click or drag for selection of non-adjacent words, the **Shift** key for ranges of text.

To edit text on the page:

1. Select the Pointer Tool, then click (or drag) in the text object. A standard insertion point appears at the click position (see below),
   - or -
   Select a single word, paragraph or portion of text.

2.   Type to insert new text or overwrite selected text, respectively.

Nulla vestibulum eleifend
nulla. Suspendisse potenti.
Aliquam turpis nisi, venenatis
non, accum san nec, imperdiet
laoreet, lacus.

To start a new paragraph:

● Press the Return key.

To start a new line within the same paragraph (using a line break or soft return):

● Press **Shift**+Return.

To flow text to the next column (Column Break), frame (Frame Break) or page (Page Break):

● Press **Ctrl**+Return, **Alt**+Return or **Ctrl+Shift**+Return, respectively.

The first two options apply only to frame text. You can use these shortcuts or choose the items from the **Insert>Break** submenu.

To switch between insert mode and overwrite mode:

● Press the **Insert** key.

Checking your text

To ensure your artistic and frame text is error-free and the best copy possible, use the **Spell Checker**, **Proof Reader**, and **Thesaurus** options on the **Tools** menu.

For paragraph indents and tab stops, see PagePlus Help or consider applying indents and tab stops as body text styles (p. 75).

Setting text properties

PagePlus gives you a high degree of typographic control over characters and paragraphs, whether you're working with frame text, table text, or artistic text.

To apply basic text formatting:

1.   Select the text.

2.   Use buttons on the Text context toolbar to change text style, font, point size, attributes, paragraph alignment, bullets/numbering, or level.

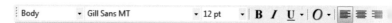

To apply paragraph formatting:

●   From the Paragraph tab, select options to control paragraph-level alignment, indent, line spacing, auto-hyphenation, and alignment to baseline grid.

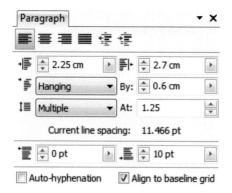

To clear local formatting (restore plain/default text properties):

1. Select a range of text with local formatting.

2. Click on the **Clear Formatting** option on the Text context toolbar's text styles drop-down list (or Text Styles tab).

Using fonts

One of the most dramatic ways to change your publication's appearance is to change the fonts used in your artistic text, frame text, or table text.

Font assignment is very simple in PagePlus, and can be done from the Text context toolbar (when text is selected), **Fonts** tab (via **View>Tabs**), or by modifying text styles (see p. 75) to use a chosen font.

Using text styles

PagePlus lets you use named **text styles** (pre-defined or user-defined), which can be applied to frame text, table text, artistic text, index text or table of contents text. A text style is a set of character and/or paragraph attributes saved as a group. When you apply a style to text, you apply the whole group of attributes in just one step. For example, you could use named paragraph styles for particular layout elements, such as "Heading

1" or "Body", and character styles to convey meaning, such as "Emphasis", "Strong", or "Subtle Reference".

Styles can be applied to characters or paragraphs using either the Text context toolbar or the Text Styles tab. Both paragraph and character styles can be managed from the **Text Style Palette**.

Paragraph and character styles

A **paragraph style** is a complete specification for the appearance of a paragraph, including all font and paragraph format attributes. Every paragraph in PagePlus has a paragraph style associated with it.

A **character style** includes only font attributes (name, point size, bold, italic, etc.), and you apply it at the character level—that is, to a range of selected characters—rather than to the whole paragraph.

Working with named styles

Body ▾ The named style of the currently selected text is displayed in either the **Text Styles** tab or the **Styles** drop-down list on the Text context toolbar. A character style (if one is applied locally) may be shown; otherwise it indicates the paragraph style.

To apply a named style:

1. Using the Pointer Tool, click in a paragraph (if applying a paragraph style) or select a range of text (if applying a character style).

2. Display the **Text Styles** tab and select a style from the style list.
   - or -
   On the Text context toolbar, click the arrow to expand the Styles drop-down list and select a style name.

The Text Style tab highlights the paragraph or character style applied to any selected text.

As both paragraph and character formatting can be applied to the same text, all of the current text's formatting is displayed in the **Current format** box on the tab. In the example below, currently selected text has a 'Strong' character style applied over a 'Body' paragraph style.

Current format: Body + Strong

To update a named style using the properties of existing text:

1. Make your desired formatting changes to any text that uses a named style.

2. On the **Text Styles** tab, right-click the style and choose **Update <style> to Match Selection**.

All text using the named style, throughout the publication, takes on the new properties.

To modify an existing style:

1. From the Text Styles tab:

    *   Right-click on the character or paragraph style you want to modify and then choose **Modify <style>**
        - or -

    *   With a style selected, select ▦ **Manage** from the **Text Styles** tab, then choose the **Modify** button.

2. From the Text Style dialog, define (or change) the style name, base style, and any character or paragraph attributes, tabs, bullets, and drop caps you want to include in the style definition.

3. Click **OK** to accept style properties, or **Cancel** to abandon changes.

4.   Click **Apply** to update text, or click **Close** to maintain the style in the publication for future use.

Alternatively, choose **Text Style Palette** from the **Format** menu to modify styles and to change text defaults (see PagePlus Help).

Creating custom text styles

If required, you can create your own custom styles, either based on a currently selected text style or from scratch. See PagePlus Help for more information.

Removing local formatting

To return characters and/or paragraphs back to their original formatting, click on **Clear Formatting** in the **Text Styles** tab. This is great for reverting some formatting which hasn't quite worked out! You can clear the formatting of selected characters, paragraphs, or both depending on what text is currently selected.

Hover over style names in your styles list, then click on a chosen style to apply the style to the selected text.

Wrapping text

PagePlus lets you wrap frame text around the contours of a separate object. Usually, this means wrapping text to a picture that overlaps or sits above a text frame. But you can wrap frame text around a shape, artistic text, table, or another frame. Wrapping is accomplished by changing the **wrap setting** for the object to which text will wrap.

Vestibulum semper enim non eros. Sed vitae arcu.
Aliquam erat volutpat. Praesent odio nisl, suscipit
at, rhoncus sit amet,
porttitor sit amet, leo.
Aenean hendrerit est.
Etiam ac augue. Morbi
tincidunt neque ut lacus.
Duis vulputate cursus
orci. Mauris justo lorem,
scelerisque sit amet, placerat sed,
condimentum in, leo. Donec urna est, semper
quis, auctor eget, ultrices in, purus. Etiam rutrum.

To wrap text around an object:

1. Select the object around which you want the text to wrap.

2. Click the 🔲 **Wrap Settings** button on the **Arrange** toolbar.

3. Select the manner in which text will wrap around the object by clicking a sample.

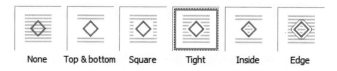

4. Choose which side(s) the chosen wrapping method will be applied, again by clicking a sample.

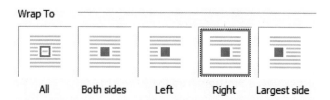

5. Click **OK**.

Creating a bulleted or numbered list

You can turn a series of paragraphs into **bulleted**, **numbered** or **multi-level lists**. Bullets are especially useful when listing items of interest in no specific order of preference, numbered lists for presenting step-by-step procedures (by number or letter), and multi-level lists for more intelligent hierarchical lists with prefixed numbers, symbols, or a mix of both, all with supporting optional text (see Using multi-level lists on p. 81).

Bulleted list	*Numbered list*	*Multi-level list*

Lists can be applied to normal text (as local formatting) or to text styles equally.

To create a simple bulleted or numbered list:

1. Select one or more paragraphs.
    - or -
    Click in a paragraph's text.

2. Select ⦙☰ **Bulleted List** or ⦙☰ **Numbered List** from the Text context toolbar.

To create a bulleted or numbered list (using presets):

1. Select one or more paragraphs.
    - or -
    Click in a paragraph's text.

2. Select **Bullets and Numbering** from the **Format** menu.

3. From the Text Style dialog's Bullets and Numbering menu option, choose **Bullet**, **Number**, or **Multi-Level** from the **Style** drop-down list.

4. Select one of the preset formats shown by default.
    - or -
    For a custom list, click the **Details** button to display, then alter custom options.

5. Click **OK** to apply list formatting.

> For number and multi-level lists, check **Restart numbering** to restart numbering from the current cursor position in the list; otherwise, leave the option unchecked.

> Click the Text context toolbar's ▭ or ▭ buttons again to turn off list formatting.

1 Vestibulum velit orci, non, leo. Nullam sed	
1.1 Lorem ipsum d elit. Suspendis	
1.2 Mauris vitae a pulvinar. Aene ornare, loborti	
1.2.1 Quisque	
1.2.2 Donec r sollicitu Maecen; malesua turpis. !	
2 In hac habitasse plate mauris. Proin mattis	
3 Proin mattis eleifend Quisque pede tellus, dictum, lectus.	

Using multi-level lists

For multi-level lists you can set a different character (symbol, text or number) to display at each level of your list. Levels are normally considered to be subordinate to each other, where Level 1 (first level), Level 2 (second), Level 3 (third), etc. are of decreasing importance in the list. For example, the simple multi-level numbered passage of text opposite is arranged at three levels.

If you apply a multi-level preset to a range of text you'll get a list with the preset's Level 1 format applied by default. Unless you use text styles, you'll have to change to levels 2, 3, 4, etc. to set the correct level for your list entry.

Changing list levels on selected paragraphs:

- Click the **Increase Paragraph Indent** or **Decrease Paragraph Indent** button on the Text context toolbar to increment or decrement the current level by one.

The multi-level presets offer some simple but commonly used schemes for paragraph list formatting. However, if you want to create your own lists or modify an existing list (your own or a preset), use the **Details** button in the Text Style dialog when Multi-Level style is selected. See PagePlus Help for more details.

Assigning bullets, numbers, and levels to styles

PagePlus lets you easily associate any bulleted, numbered or multi-level list style (either preset or custom list) to an existing text style. See Using text styles on p. 75.

Inserting user details

When you create a publication from a design template for the first time, you may be prompted to update your user details (Name, Company, Telephone number, etc.) in a User Details dialog. These details will automatically populate pre-defined text "fields" in your publication, making it personalized.

PagePlus supports business sets (i.e., stored sets of user details) which can be created per customer and applied to your publication. This lets you create publication variants, with each differing just in their user details. You can choose which set to use when you start with a new design template (or at any time during your session).

To add, edit or change user details:

1. Click the  **User Details** button on the Pages context toolbar (deselect objects to view).

2. Enter new information into the spaces on the **Business Sets** or **Home** tab (a **Calendars** tab will appear if there is a calendar in your publication).

3. Click **Update**.

If you're starting from scratch, you need to have user details fields placed in your publication.

Inserting your own fields

You can also insert one or more User Details fields into any publication at any time.

To insert a User Detail field:

1. Select the Pointer Tool and click in the text for an insertion point.

2. From the **Insert** menu, select **Information>User Details**.

3. Select a user detail entry and optionally any text **Prefix** or **Suffix** to include with your user details, e.g. *(Home) Name*.

4. Click **OK**.

For existing publications, the fields (once edited) can be updated or swapped as described previously.

To swap user detail fields:

1. On the page, select the user detail field you want to swap out.

2. Click the 📷 icon on the control bar above the selected field.

3. In the dialog, select an entry to insert, e.g. *(Home) Name,* and optionally any text **Prefix** or **Suffix** to include with your user details.

4. Click **OK**.

Creating business sets

To create a new business set:

1. On the User Details dialog, click **New**.

2. Fill in the empty user details fields.

To swap to a new business set:

• Select an alternative set from the **Select Set** drop-down list, then click **Update**.

Tables, Charts, and Calendars

6

Creating tables

Tables are ideal for presenting text and data in a variety of easily customizable row-and-column formats, with built-in spreadsheet capabilities.

Rather than starting from scratch, PagePlus is supplied with a selection of pre-defined table formats, called **AutoFormats**, that can be used. Simply pick one and fill in the cells with content.

PagePlus lets you:

- Edit the pre-defined format before adding a new table to the page.

- Design your own custom formats without creating a table. See Creating custom table formats in PagePlus Help.

- Quickly create custom formats based on the selected table.

- Edit existing tables to fit a different format (pre-defined or custom).

To create a table:

1. On the **Tools** toolbar, choose the **Table Tool** from the ▾ **Table** flyout.

2. Click on the page or pasteboard, or drag to set the table's dimensions. The **Create Table** dialog opens with a selection of preset table formats shown in the **Format** window.

3. Step through the list to preview the layouts and select one. To begin with a plain table, select (**Default**).

4. Set the **Table Size**. This is the number of rows and columns that make up the table layout.

5. Click **OK**. The new table appears on the page.

> Plan your table layout in advance, considering the number of rows/columns needed!

Flowing tables

It is possible to create tables that can be split into multiple parts on the same page or even across multiple pages. This is useful if you're planning to present a large amount of table data or if you're constrained by your existing page design; for either reason, table placement becomes that much easier.

Region	J	F	M	A	M	J
N	12	8	7	9	11	8
S	6	6	7	10	14	12
W	12	6	5	20	9	18

J	A	S	O	N	D	Sum
18	11	3	11	22	16	136
11	13	7	13	14	10	123
17	14	10	14	13	18	156

Even though physically split, each table portion still maintains a link with previous and next tables. This allows additional rows or columns to be added, with the table reflowing subsequent rows or columns.

You can design your flowing table from scratch or split up an existing table already on the page.

To create a flowing table from scratch:

1. Create your table as described in To create a table (p. 87).

2. On the control bar under your selected table, click **Flow Down** to create a linked table based on extra rows, or **Flow Right** for a linked table based on extra columns.

If you've a table that you've created previously or you're redesigning your table layout, you can split it by row or column.

To split up an existing flowing table:

1. Select the table.

2. Hover over arrows shown at table bottom-centre or right-centre.

3. Drag these arrows up or left, respectively, to split by row or column.

The rows or columns hidden by dragging will pop up as a linked table on mouse release.

To navigate between linked tables:

- Under your selected table, click **Next Table** or **Previous Table**.

To rejoin tables:

1. Select a linked table to which you want to rejoin the next table in the linked sequence.

2. On the control bar, click **Rejoin**.

For flowing tables it's a great idea to repeat the initial table's row or column headers on each linked table. This is essential for correct referencing of table data.

Row or column headers are repeated on all linked tables based on extra rows (Flow down) or columns (Flow right). You can't repeat row and column headers in the same linked table sequence.

To repeat row/column headers:

1. Select the initial table in the table flow.

2. Click the drop-down arrow, displayed on hover over in the row/column header (shown as '1' and 'A' below).

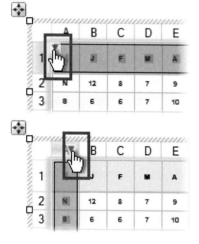

3. Select **Repeat as Header** from the submenu. The row or column header is repeated on the linked table.

Using charts

For any small business, club, or school project, the ability to present important data professionally will impress your audience, and potentially gain support for your activities.

Tables and charts are intrinsically linked in PagePlus. If you need a recap on tables, see Creating tables on p. 87. PagePlus also lets you create multiple charts from the same table data using the **Chart Data** tab. See Manipulating chart data (in PagePlus Help) for more information.

Chart types

PagePlus provides a range of popular chart types, each designed to present data differently. All you need to do is select a chart that suits the type of data you wish to present.

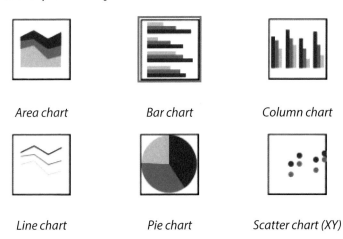

Area chart	*Bar chart*	*Column chart*
Line chart	*Pie chart*	*Scatter chart (XY)*

The above chart types are also available in 3D (as extrusions of the 2D chart types).

Charts explained

Charts are made up of specific elements. Once you learn how to manipulate each element using the **Charts** tab and **Chart Data** tab, you'll be able to create powerful charts easily.

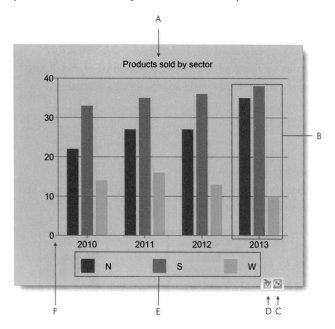

*(**A**) Chart Title, (**B**) Series, (**C**) Go to Chart Data link, (**D**) Go to Associated Table link, (**E**) Series Legend, (**F**) Chart Area.*

Data sources

The first step in creating charts is to consider what data you'll want to base your chart on. You should spend some time in advance preparing data for chart presentation.

Several data sources can be used to base your chart on. Here's an overview of typical data sources that will let you create charts easily.

Data source	Description
Chart Data tab	Using PagePlus's Chart Data tab, you can either: • Create your own off-the-page chart data without the need for a PagePlus table. See Creating charts from scratch on p. 93. -or - • Create chart variations (of differing type and data ranges) from a single PagePlus table. For more details, see Manipulating chart data (in PagePlus Help) for more information.
PagePlus table	If you have a PagePlus publication which already has a table present, you can base your chart on that table data, with the option of presenting table and chart data in unison.
External spreadsheet	You can paste cell data from Microsoft Excel directly onto your page or pasteboard. Once in PagePlus, you can create a chart as you would with a PagePlus table.

 If you want to use table data from Microsoft Word, copy and paste the table into Excel first.

Creating charts from scratch

PagePlus provides the **Chart Tool** to place a chart onto your page. Initially a placeholder chart, it can be populated with real chart data from the **Chart Data** tab. The tab lets you store and develop your chart data "off-page" without cluttering up your page design.

The chart can be designed and later modified by using a Chart context toolbar displayed above your workspace when the chart is selected.

To create a chart from scratch:

1. From the **Tools** toolbar's ⊞ ▼ **Table Tools** flyout, select ▮▮ **Chart Tool**.

2. On the context toolbar, from the **Chart** drop-down list, select a chart type.

3. Click on the page or drag out the chart to the desired size.

At this point, the chart is just a placeholder, using sample data automatically added to the **Chart Data** tab. You can edit this sample data using your own data, name your row/column headers, and even add extra rows and columns to suit additional chart data—by default, each row represents a separate colour-coded series component.

To edit data in the Chart Data tab:

1. Click ▦ **Chart Data** under the selected chart.

    The Chart Data tab displays temporarily in the workspace.

2. On the **Chart Data** tab, click in each cell and enter data as appropriate.

    The chart will update with the newly entered values.

3. Replace the row and numeric column headers (i.e., Series 1, 2, and 3; and 1, 2, 3, 4, respectively) with real names. These will update in your chart immediately.

Modifying charts

It is possible that you may want to change how your chart is presented. The Chart context toolbar gives you the freedom to swap between chart types, base your chart on different ranges, and toggle series as row or columns.

Editing titles

To edit your chart title:

- Click on the chart title and begin typing.

Formatting and styling charts

To display the Charts tab:

- At the bottom of your right-hand tab group, click **Charts**.

The tab offers three buttons called Chart, Axes, and Series.

- **Chart**: Used for title and series legend control and positioning. Other options are the same as provided on the Chart context toolbar.

- **Axes**: The Axes section adds axis-specific titles, labels, guides, and any other chart elements that aid the interpretation of chart data.

- **Series**: Modifies individual series, including manually assigning series labels, series plotting, enabling trend lines, error bars, and value labels.

For an easy way to transform your chart's appearance in one click, you can use the Styles tab.

To apply a style to your chart:

1. On the **Styles** tab, select the **Charts** category from the drop-down list.

2. Click on a style preset thumbnail.

Inserting a calendar

The **Calendar Wizard** helps you design month-at-a-glance calendars for use in your publication, with optional addition of personal events and public holidays.

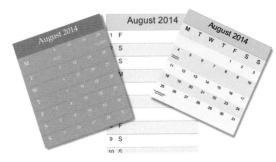

The calendar is created as a scalable text-based table so you can edit text using the standard text tools. The properties of a selected calendar are similar to those of a table, and can be modified identically (see Manipulating tables in PagePlus Help). Like custom table formats you can create your own custom calendar formats.

To insert a calendar:

1. Click the Table flyout on the **Tools** toolbar and choose 	 **Insert Calendar**.

2. Click again on your page, or drag out to set the calendar size.

3. From the displayed **Calendar Wizard**, define options for your calendar. To have your country's public holidays shown, check **Add public holidays** in the wizard and select a **Region** from the associated drop-down list. To add personal events, check **Add personal events** additionally.

4. Click **Finish** to complete the wizard.

To view and edit a selected calendar's properties:

• Click 	 **Edit Calendar** on the Calendar context toolbar.

Pictures

Adding picture frames

Picture frames let you present your pictures in a decorative surround, much like you'd show off your favourite picture in a picture frame in your home. You can select from an impressive collection of professionally designed picture frames, and simply drag them onto your publication page before filling them with pictures.

> Picture frames are assets, along with graphics, pictures, page elements, backgrounds, and are browsed for (and managed) in the same way as any other asset. See Using assets on p. 47.

To add a picture frame:

1. From the Assets tab, select **Browse**.

2. In the **Asset Browser** dialog, select **Picture Frames** from the **Categories** section.

3. Navigate the themed sub-categories to locate a picture frame, then select an individual frame or click **Add All** 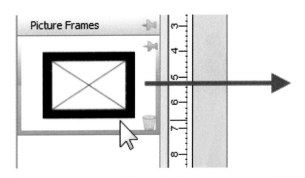 to include all the frames from the sub-category. A check mark will appear on selected thumbnails.

4. Click **Close**. The frame(s) appears in the **Assets** tab (Picture Frames category).

5. Drag a chosen frame thumbnail to your page.

> Empty picture frames are shown as envelope-shaped placeholders on the page.

To add a borderless picture frame:

1. Select **Rectangular Picture Frame** on the **Tools** toolbar's **Picture** flyout.
   - or -
   Select **Picture>Empty Frame** from the **Insert** menu.

2. The mouse pointer changes to the **Picture Paste** cursor. What you do next determines the initial size and placement of the picture frame.

   - To insert the frame at a default size, simply click the mouse.
     - or -

- To set the size of the frame, drag out a region and release the mouse button. If needed, use the Shift key while dragging to maintain aspect ratio (to a square).

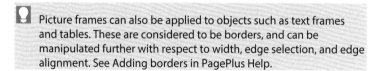

Picture frames can also be applied to objects such as text frames and tables. These are considered to be borders, and can be manipulated further with respect to width, edge selection, and edge alignment. See Adding borders in PagePlus Help.

To add a picture to a frame (and vice versa):

- From the Assets tab (Pictures category), drag and drop a picture directly onto the picture frame. - or -

- From the Assets tab (Picture Frames category), drag and drop a picture frame directly onto an already placed picture.

The picture is added to the frame using default Picture Frame properties, i.e. it is scaled to maximum fit; aspect ratio is always maintained. However, you can alter the picture's size, orientation, positioning, and scaling relative to its frame.

Creating shaped picture frames

While you can take advantage of PagePlus's preset frames you can create your own shape (e.g., a morphed QuickShape or closed curve) then convert it to a picture frame.

To create a shaped picture frame:

1. Create a closed shape or QuickShapes.

2. Right-click the shape and select **Convert To>Picture Frame**.

You can then add a picture to the frame as described previously.

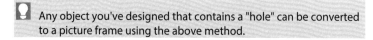

Any object you've designed that contains a "hole" can be converted to a picture frame using the above method.

To store the picture frame for reuse globally or just in the publication, drag to the Assets tab's My Designs or Picture Frames category. For the latter, if you close the publication, you'll be asked if you want to save the frame to an asset pack. See Storing designs in PagePlus Help.

Adding pictures

The **Assets** tab (Pictures category) acts as a "basket" for initially gathering together and then including pictures in your publication. Its chief use is to aid the design process by improving efficiency (avoiding having to import pictures one by one) and convenience (making pictures always-at-hand). For picture-rich publications in particular, the tab is a valuable tool for dragging pictures directly into bordered or unbordered picture frames or for simply replacing existing pictures on the page.

PagePlus also lets you insert pictures of a wide variety of file formats, such as bitmaps, vector images, and metafiles (including Serif Metafiles).

 PDF files can also be placed as non-editable graphics. When placed as graphics, PDFs be moved, rotated, cropped and recoloured like normal images, but cannot be edited using PhotoLab, the Cutout Studio, or an external image editing program. To edit PDFs in PagePlus they need to be opened or inserted as editable documents.

For photos from your digital camera, you can simply navigate to the folder containing your already downloaded photos (i.e., on your hard disk) and include them in the tab. Similarly, scanned images already saved to your hard disk can be added by this method.

Adding pictures to the Assets tab

To add pictures to the tab:

1. Select the Assets tab's Pictures category, and click **Add.**

2. From the dialog, navigate to a folder, and select your picture(s).

3. Click **Open**. Your pictures appear as thumbnails within the Assets tab's Picture category.

To reorder pictures in the tab:

- Select and drag a picture to a new position in the tab.

To delete a picture from the tab:

- Hover over the bottom-right corner of the picture thumbnail and click the 🗑 icon.

To delete selected pictures:

1. **Ctrl**-click or **Shift**-click to select non-adjacent or adjacent pictures.

2. Right-click any selected picture, and select **Delete Assets**.

To delete all pictures:

- Right-click any picture and select **Delete All**.

Adding pictures to the page

Pictures can be added to your publication by dragging directly onto your page.

To add a picture to your page:

- From the Assets tab (Pictures category), drag a picture thumbnail directly onto the page, inline into artistic/frame text (at a chosen insertion point), or into a picture frame. Once added, the picture thumbnail indicates the number of times the picture has been used in the publication (①).

If you've positioned empty picture frames you can use **AutoFlow** to automatically populate them with pictures.

AutoFlow—adding content automatically

AutoFlow lets you flow the pictures present in the tab's Pictures category throughout empty picture **frames** spread throughout your publication (you can't reflow pictures once frames are populated with content).

To automatically flow your pictures:

- Click **AutoFlow** at the bottom of the Assets tab (Pictures category). The pictures are placed sequentially in your document's available picture frames in the order they appear in the tab (reorder beforehand if needed).

Searching for tagged pictures

PagePlus lets you retrieve pictures by individual **tag**, i.e. XMP metadata stored within each picture. You can tag photos by using the Asset Manager.

To search for pictures by tag:

- Click in the search box at the bottom of the Assets tab and enter a search term, e.g. holiday. Matching pictures will appear directly above the search box in a temporary Search Results tab.

Adding pictures with resizing and embed/link control

As well as dragging a picture thumbnail from the Assets tab, pictures can be added to PagePlus by copy and paste or dragging a file from an external Windows folder directly onto your page.

PagePlus also lets you import pictures via 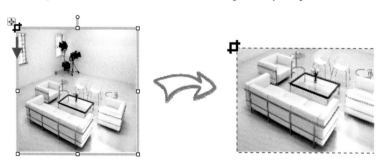 **Import Picture** on the **Tools** toolbar. You'll be able to size the picture and embed or link it.

Cropping pictures

PagePlus includes the **Square Crop Tool** and **Irregular Crop Tool** which are used typically for cropping pictures on the page. Cropping discards unwanted "outer" regions of a picture while keeping the remainder visible.

To crop a selected picture (square crop):

1. On the **Attributes** toolbar, click the **Square Crop Tool**.

2. Hover over an edge/ corner handle until you see a crop cursor.

3. Drag the cursor inwards (down, left or right) on your picture.

4. Repeat with other edge or corner handles, if needed.

5. (Optional) From the context toolbar, set a **Feather** value to add a soft edge to your picture.

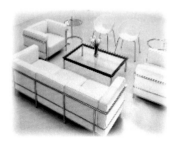

To crop a picture (irregular crop)

1. With the ⬜ **Square Crop Tool** selected, select the ◣ **Irregular Crop Tool** above your workspace.

2. The Curve context toolbar appears on its right, which lets you control the displayed nodes and connecting segments that define the object's crop outline. See Editing lines in PagePlus Help.

    *   To move a node (control point) where you see the ⊣⊢ cursor, drag the node.

    *   ▶∿ To move a line segment (between two nodes) where you see the cursor, drag the segment.

3. Add extra nodes by double-clicking on the crop outline, then reposition them.

> 💡 To scale the object within the crop outline, press the **Ctrl** key, click your left mouse button, then move your mouse upwards or downwards.

If you add picture frames to your publication, you can position your placed picture using pan and zoom instead of using the Square Crop Tool.

Cropping pictures to shapes

The **Crop to Shape** command lets you create shaped pictures from drawn closed shapes (below) or silhouettes placed over your picture. The picture gets clipped to the outline of the shape, leaving a shape equivalent to the overlapping region.

To crop a picture using shapes:

1. Place the shape in front of the picture to be cropped, using the **Arrange** menu and/or **Arrange** toolbar as needed.

2. With both objects selected (or grouped), choose **Crop to Shape** from the **Tools** menu.

You can restore an object cropped in this way to its original shape, but the upper "cropping" object is permanently deleted (use **Undo** to recover it if necessary).

Using Cutout Studio

Cutout Studio offers a powerful integrated solution for cutting objects out from their backgrounds. Depending on the make up of your images you can separate subject of interests from their backgrounds, either by retaining the subject of interest (usually people, objects, etc.) or removing a simple uniform background (e.g., sky, studio backdrop). In both instances, the resulting "cutout" image creates an eye-catching look for your publication.

The initial green background is discarded, leaving interim checkerboard transparency, from which another image can be used as a more attractive background. A red tint on the second image's background is used to indicate areas to be discarded.

To launch Cutout Studio:

1. Select a picture to be cut out.

2. Select **Cutout Studio** from the displayed Picture context toolbar. Cutout Studio is launched.

Choose an output

By default an alpha-edged bitmap is created by cutting out, but's possible to change the **Output Type** prior to selecting areas for keeping/discarding.

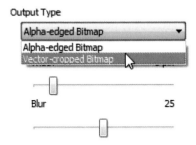

The choice you make really depends on the picture. A vector-edged bitmap is better for cutting out pictures with well defined edges.

 Zoom into your image to examine its edges; this may influence the output type chosen.

Selecting areas to keep or discard

A pair of brushes for keeping and discarding is used to "paint" areas of the image. The tools are called **Keep Brush** and **Discard Brush**, and are either used independently or, more typically, in combination with each other. When using either tool, the brush paints an area contained by an outline which is considered to be retained or discarded (depending on brush type). A configurable number of pixels adjacent to the outline area are blended.

To select image areas for keeping/discarding:

1.   In Cutout Studio, click either   **Keep Brush Tool** or
     Discard Brush Tool from the left of the Studio workspace.

2. (Optional) Pick a **Brush size** suitable for the area to be worked on.

3. (Optional) Set a **Grow Tolerance** value to automatically expand the selected area under the cursor (by detecting colours similar to those within the current selection). The greater the value the more the selected area will grow. Uncheck the option to switch the feature off.

4. Using the circular cursor, click and drag across the area to be retained or discarded (depending on Keep or Discard Brush Tool selection). It's OK to repeatedly click and drag until your selection area is made.

   The ![undo icon] **Undo** button reverts to the last made selection.

5. If you're outputting an alpha-edged bitmap, you can refine the area to be kept/discarded within Cutout Studio (only after previewing) with Erase and Restore touch-up tools. Vector-cropped images can be cropped using standard PagePlus crop tools outside of the Studio.

6. Click ![ok icon] **OK** to create your cutout.

PhotoLab filters and retouching tools

PhotoLab is a powerful studio for applying adjustment and effect filters to pictures individually or in combination—all instantly applied and previewed—and carrying out popular edits like image straightening!

PhotoLab hosts filter tabs, a main toolbar, and applied filter stack around a central workspace.

A   B   C

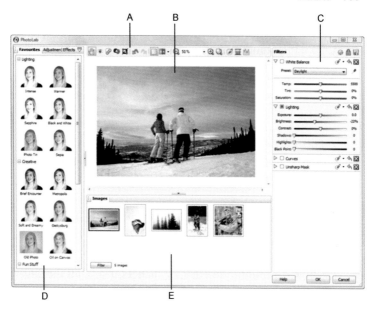

D   E

*(**A**) Main toolbar, (**B**) Main workspace, (**C**) Filter stack, (**D**) Filter tabs, (**E**) Images tab*

To launch PhotoLab:

1. Select the picture that you want to apply a filter to.

2. Click **PhotoLab** on the Picture context toolbar.

Applying a filter

Filters are stored in PhotoLab's Favourites, Adjustments, and Effects tabs which group filters logically into categories (e.g., Quick Fix for fast and commonly used correction filters).

The Favourites tab offers some commonly used filters (individual and in combination). You can complement these with your own user-defined filters.

To preview, fine tune, and apply a filter:

1. Click a filter thumbnail.

2. As soon as a filter is selected it is temporarily added to **Trial Zone** which lets you experiment freely with your own settings for that filter.

3. Adjust sliders (or enter input values) until your filter suits your requirements. Some filters offer check boxes, drop-down lists, and additional controls (e.g., Advanced settings).

> Selecting a new filter always replaces the current filter.

To commit your filter:

*   Click ⊖ **Commit** to accept your changes. This adds the filter to the right-most **Filters** stack where additional filters can be added and built up by using the same method.

Effects and Styles

8

Applying effects

PagePlus provides a variety of **effects** that you can use to enhance any object. 2D effects such as drop shadows, feather, bevels, emboss are popular, along with 3D effects for more sophisticated textured surface effects.

Both 2D and 3D effects can be applied individually (or in combination) using the **Effects tab**.

2D effects

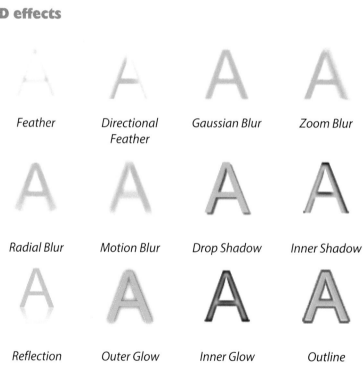

Feather	*Directional Feather*	*Gaussian Blur*	*Zoom Blur*
Radial Blur	*Motion Blur*	*Drop Shadow*	*Inner Shadow*
Reflection	*Outer Glow*	*Inner Glow*	*Outline*

Inner Bevel   Outer Bevel   Emboss   Pillow Emboss

Colour Fill   Trail

To apply 2D effects:

1. Select an object.

2. Display the Effects tab by clicking its tab name (presented vertically at the right of your screen by default).

• To switch on Feather, Drop Shadow, or Outer Glow, click the effect's ☐ icon. The effect's default settings are displayed.
   - or -

   i. For other effects, click ⚙ **Choose Effects** at the top of the tab.

   ii. From the flyout, select **2D Effects** and select an effect from the submenu. The effect is added to the tab, and its entry in the flyout will be checked.

3. Adjust settings by altering sliders, values, check boxes, or drop-down lists. Drag left or right over values to adjust.

As you change settings, the effect on the page updates automatically.

To switch off an effect:

- Click the effect's icon on its title bar. Note that your adjusted settings are kept but are switched off.

To reset an effect back to default:

- Click the effect's ↰ icon on its title bar.

To remove an effect from the tab:

- Click ⚙ **Choose Effects** at the top of the tab, then click to uncheck the effect's entry on the flyout. If the effect is applied to a selected object(s) it will be removed from the object.

Using favourites

To apply effects using favourites:

1. On the Effects tab, click ✯ **Favourites** on the chosen effect's title bar.

2. On the displayed gallery, select an effect thumbnail.

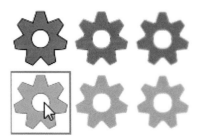

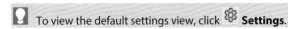 To view the default settings view, click ⚙ **Settings**.

To save a custom effect to your favourites:

1. Adjust settings for your chosen effect.

2. On the effect's title bar, click 🌟 **Add Favourite**. Your effect is saved to the favourites gallery.

3D Effects

3D effects go beyond 2D effects (such as shadow, glow, bevel, and emboss effects) to create the impression of a textured surface on the object itself. You can use the **Effects** tab to apply one or more 3D effects to the same object.

You'll find that some effects are used in combination to create realistic surface effects such as glass.

To apply 3D effects:

1. Select an object.

2. Display the Effects tab by clicking its tab name (presented vertically at the right of your screen by default).

3. Click 🌀 **Choose Effects** at the top of the tab.

4. From the flyout, select **3D Effects** and select an effect from the submenu. The effect is added to the tab.

5. Add further effects from the flyout depending on the type of effect you want.

6. Adjust settings for 3D effects by altering sliders, values, check boxes, or drop-down lists. Drag left or right over values to adjust.

> The **3D Effects & Lighting** category hosts master control settings which are enabled when any 3D effect is applied.

> For a detailed description of each effect's settings, see PagePlus Help (Effects tab topic).

Using the Shadow Tool

Shadows are great for adding flair and dimension to your work, particularly to pictures and text objects, but also to shapes, text frames and tables. To help you create them quickly and easily, PagePlus provides the **Shadow Tool** on the **Attributes** toolbar. The tool affords freeform control of the shadow effect directly on the page.

For more creative shadows, the tool lets you apply skewed shadows, again directly on the page.

Adjustment of shadow colour, opacity, blur, and scaling/distance is possible using controllable nodes directly on the page (or via a supporting Shadow context toolbar).

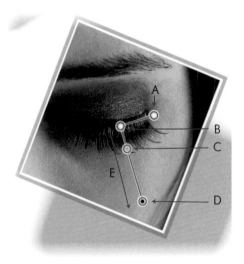

(A) Blur, (B) Shadow origin, (C) Opacity, (D) Colour, (E) Scaling

Once you've created a shadow, you can also fine-tune it as needed using the **Effects** tab.

Using object styles

The **Styles** tab contains multiple galleries of pre-designed styles that you can apply to any object, or customize to suit your own taste! Galleries exist in effect categories including Blurs, 3D, Edge, Warps, Materials and more, with each category having further subcategories.

3D surface and texture presets are available in various categories (Presets - Default, Presets - Fun, Presets - Materials, and Texture). The Presets - Materials category offers realistic effects such as Glass, Metallic, Wood, etc.

> Styles store fill, transparency, line/text properties, and effects under a single style name, making it easy to apply combinations of attributes to an object in one click.

At a later date, if you edit the style, all objects using the original style will update automatically to the new style definition.

To apply an object style to a selected object(s):

1. Display the **Styles** tab.

2. Expand the drop-down menu to select a named style category (e.g., Presets - Default), then pick a subcategory (e.g., Mixed) by scrolling the lower window.

3. Preview available styles as thumbnails (cog shapes are shown by default) in the window.

4. Click a style thumbnail to apply that style.

To unlink an object from its style definition:

- Right-click the object and choose **Format>Object Style>Unlink**.

To create a custom object style:

- Right-click the object and choose **Format>Object Style>Create**.

See Creating custom object styles in PagePlus Help for more information.

Colour, Fills, and Transparency

9

Applying solid fills

PagePlus offers a number of ways to apply solid colour fills to objects of different kinds:

- You can apply solid colours to an object's **line** or **fill**. As you might expect, QuickShapes and closed shapes have both line and fill properties, whereas straight and freehand lines have only a line property.

- Characters in text objects can have a background fill, line, and text colour (i.e., for highlighting, text outlines, and the text fill itself). Text frames and table cells can have a background fill independent of the characters they contain.

To apply a solid colour via the Colour tab or Swatches tab:

1. Select the object(s) or highlight a range of text.

2. Select the appropriate tab, then click the ⬜ **Fill**, ⬜ **Line**, or **A** **Text** button at the top of the tab to determine where colour will be applied. The colour of the underline reflects the colour of your selected object.

3. For the Colour tab, select a colour from the colour spectrum or sliders depending on colour mode selected.

   - or -

   ▪▪ ▪▪ ▾ For the Swatches tab, select a colour swatch from the **Publication palette** (commonly used colours and those previously applied to your publication) or a specific themed or standard **Palette** (supplied preset swatches).

Alternatively, use **Format>Fill** to apply colour via a dialog.

Using the **Colours** toolbar, you can reapply the last applied fill, line, or text colour and also predefine these colours for future objects. By default, the toolbar is always in view thus aiding design productivity.

To apply the last applied solid colour:

1. Select the object(s) or highlight a range of text.

2. 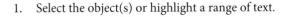 On the **Colours** toolbar, select the **Fill**, **Line**, or **Text** button.

To predefine colours for future objects:

•   With no objects selected, click the down arrow on the toolbar's **Fill**, **Line**, or **Text** buttons and choose a colour from the menu, This is equivalent to using the Colour or Swatches tab.

To change a solid colour's shade/tint (lightness):

1. Select the object and set the correct Fill, Line or Text button in the **Colour** tab.

2. From the Colour mode drop-down list, select **Tinting**.

3. Drag the Shade/Tint slider to the left or right to darken or lighten your starting colour, respectively. You can also enter a value between -100 and 100 in the box. Entering 0 in the input box reverts to the original colour.

Adjust the 18% percentage tinting via slider or direct input to apply object tinting from the **Swatches** tab.

PagePlus automatically adds used colours to the 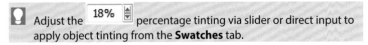 **Publication Palette** available in the **Swatches** tab and **Fill** dialog.

You can convert any colour in your palette into a spot colour by selecting the colour's swatch and the **Spot Colour** checkbox in **Palette Manager** (available from the **Tools** menu).

To change the current palette:

- On the **Swatches** tab, click the ![icon] ▾ **Palette** button to view and adopt colours from a **Standard RGB**, **Standard CMYK**, or selection of themed palettes. Colours can be added, edited, or deleted from the Publication Palette but not from other palettes.

Replacing colours

In PagePlus, changing all instances of a regular colour in your publication is as easy as updating a scheme colour.

This can be very useful when you have designed a publication without using scheme colours and change your mind (or a client does) about which colours to use, altering colours without manually selecting and changing each object. This can also be of benefit when editing a PDF that requires document-wide colour changes, and when choosing to turn regular colours into scheme colours.

Replace a colour in the publication palette

1. In the Swatches tab, click the down arrow on the ![icon] ▾ **Publication palette** button and select **Publication Palette**.

2. Right-click on the colour you want to replace and choose **Replace Colour** from the menu.

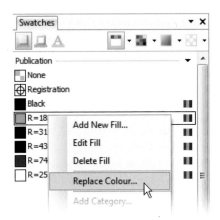

3. Choose the new colour using one of the many colour models, palettes, pickers, and scheme colours available in the **Colour Selector** dialog.

4. Click **OK** to apply the new colour in place of the old.

Using colour schemes

In PagePlus, a **colour scheme** is a cluster of eleven complementary colours (of which **five** are mainly used) that you can apply to specific elements in one or more publications. The **Schemes** tab displays preset schemes (displaying the five main colours) which can be selected at any point during the design process.

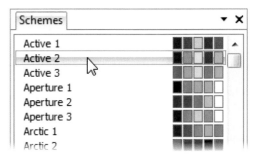

Each publication can have just one colour scheme at a time; the current scheme is highlighted in the **Schemes** tab. You can easily switch schemes, modify scheme colours and create custom schemes. Colour schemes are saved globally, so the full set of schemes is always available.

How colour schemes work

Colour schemes in PagePlus work much like a paint-by-numbers system, where various regions of a layout are coded with numbers, and a specific colour is assigned (by number) to each region. For example, imagine a line drawing coded with the numbers 1 through 5. To fill it in, you'd use paint from jars also numbered 1 through 5. Swapping different colours into the paint jars, while keeping the numbers on the drawing the same, would produce quite a different painting.

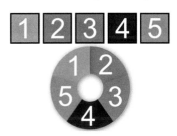

In PagePlus, the "paint jars" are numbers you can assign to objects in your publication. They're known as "Scheme Colour 1," "Scheme Colour 2," and so on. When you apply Scheme Colour 1 to an object, it's like saying, "Put the colour from jar number 1 here."

The **Schemes** tab shows the various available schemes, each with a different set of five colours in the five "jars." Whichever named colour scheme you select, that scheme's first colour (as shown in its sample) will appear in regions defined as Scheme Colour 1, its second colour will map to Scheme Colour 2, and so on throughout the publication.

To select a colour scheme:

1. Click the **Schemes** tab. The currently assigned scheme is highlighted in the list.

2. Click a different colour scheme sample. Objects in the publication that have been assigned one of the colour scheme numbers are updated with the corresponding colour from the new scheme.

 By default, the Schemes tab is collapsed at the bottom right of the workspace.

You can repeat this selection process indefinitely. When you save a publication, its current colour scheme is saved along with the document.

Applying scheme colours to objects

When you create publications from pre-defined design templates (see p. 15), you can choose the starting colour scheme that you want to adopt; you can always change it later from the **Schemes** tab. This flexibility creates endless possibilities for the look and feel of your publication! However, if you then create new elements in your schemed publication, or start a publication from scratch, how can you extend the current colour scheme to the new objects? Although you'll need to spend some time working out which colour combinations look best, the mechanics of the process are simple. Recalling the paint-by-numbers example above, all you need to do is assign one of the current scheme colour numbers to an object's line and/or fill.

To assign a scheme colour to an object:

1. On the **Swatches** tab, from the **Publications Palette** flyout, select **Scheme Colours**.

The palette displays only scheme colours.

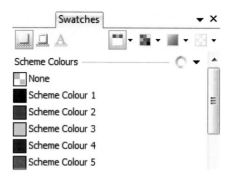

2.   Select the object and choose a 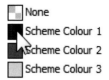 **Fill**, **Line**, or **Text**
     button at the top of the **Swatches** tab depending on the desired
     effect.

3.   Click on the scheme colour that you want to apply to the fill, line, or
     text.

If an object's fill uses a scheme colour, the corresponding sample in
Swatches tab will be highlighted whenever the object is selected.

PagePlus also allows you to modify any existing colour scheme and create your own scheme from a colour spread. See PagePlus Help for more information.

Gradient and bitmap fills

Gradient fills provide a gradation or spectrum of colours spreading between two or more points on an object. A gradient fill has an editable path with handles that mark the origin of each of these key colours. A bitmap fill uses a named bitmap—often a material, pattern, or background image—to fill an object.

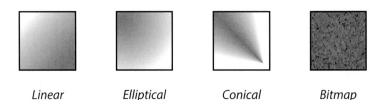

| *Linear* | *Elliptical* | *Conical* | *Bitmap* |

You can apply preset gradient and bitmap fills from the Swatches tab to the fill or outline of a shape or text frame. Table cells as well as artistic, frame, and table text can also take a gradient or bitmap fill. The fill's path on an object's fill or line can also be varied for different effects (see PagePlus Help).

Applying a gradient or bitmap fill

There are several ways to apply a gradient or bitmap fill: using the **Swatches** tab, the **Fill Tool**, or the **Fill** dialog.

PagePlus can also produce automatic gradient fills based on applied solid colours—giving you an almost unlimited number of gradient fill choices.

The easiest way to apply a gradient or bitmap fill is to use one of a range of pre-supplied swatch thumbnails in the Swatches tab's **Gradient** or **Bitmap** palettes. The **Fill Tool**, **Fill** dialog and **Edit Fill** dialog are alternative methods for applying and editing gradient fills.

To apply an automatic gradient:

1. Select an object with a solid colour applied to its fill, outline, and/or text.

2. Using the Colour toolbar's **Fill**, **Line** or **Text** buttons, select an automatic gradient that blends from the current colour to white or black.

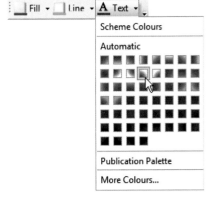

To apply a preset gradient or bitmap fill using the Swatches tab:

1.    Display the Swatches tab and ensure either **Fill, Line**, or **Text** is selected (for an object's fill, outline, or text fill respectively).

     Note that the colour of the underline reflects the colour of your selected object.

2.   For gradient fills, select a gradient category, e.g. Linear, Elliptical, etc., from the **Gradient** button's drop-down list.
     - or -

     For bitmap fills, select a drop-down list category from the **Bitmap** button.

3.   Select the object(s), and then click the appropriate gallery swatch for the fill you want to apply.
     - or -

     Drag a gallery swatch onto any object (it doesn't need to be selected) and release the mouse button. This will affect the object's Fill but not its Line or Text fill.

4.   If needed, adjust the fill's **Tint** at the bottom of the tab with the tab slider or set a percentage value in the input box.

     Applying different transparency effects (using the **Transparency** tab) won't alter the object's fill settings as such, but may significantly alter a fill's actual appearance.

To apply a gradient fill with the Fill Tool:

1.   Select an object.

2.   Click the **Fill Tool** on the **Attributes** toolbar.

3.  Display the Swatches tab and ensure either **Fill**, **Line**, or **Text** is selected (for an object's fill, outline, or text fill respectively). The colour of the underline reflects the colour of your selected object.

4. Click and drag on the object to define the fill path. The object takes a simple Linear fill, grading from the object's current colour to monochrome white.

If the object is white already (or has no fill), grading is from white to black.

You can modify the gradient further using the context toolbar.

To modify a gradient start and end colours using the context toolbar:

1. With the object selected, click the  **Fill Tool** on the **Attributes** toolbar.

2. On the context toolbar:

   • Choose the fill type from the drop-down list. (You can also apply a **Solid** or **None** fill type.)

- From the 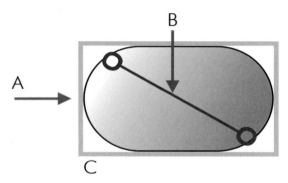 **Start Colour** drop-down list, select a colour or click **More Colours** to display the **Colour Selector** dialog.

  You can also apply an **End Colour** in the same way.
  - or -

  For **Three** or **Four Colour** only, select an object's fill handle and select a colour from the **Fill Colour** drop-down list.

Alternatively, a dialog can be used to add or subtract **key colours** from the gradient, apply different key colours to individual handles, or vary the overall shading of the effect applied to the object.

Editing the fill path

When you select a fillable object, the **Fill Tool** becomes available (otherwise it's greyed out). When you select the Fill Tool, if the object uses a **gradient fill**, you'll see the **fill path** displayed as a line, with handles marking where the spectrum between each key colour begins and ends. Adjusting the handle positions determines the actual spread of colours between handles. You can also edit a gradient fill by adding, deleting, or changing key colours.

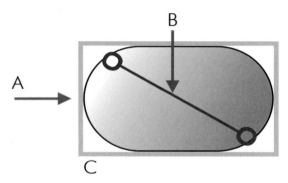

(A) Linear Fill based on key colours, (B) Path, (C) Effect on Object

To adjust the gradient fill path on a selected object:

1.   ▁ ▁ **A** Display the Swatches tab and ensure either **Fill**, **Line**, or **Text** is selected (for an object's fill, outline, or text fill respectively).

     Note that the colour of the underline reflects the colour of your selected object.

2.   Click the ◇ **Fill Tool** on the **Attributes** toolbar. The fill path appears on the object's fill, outline, or text content.

3.   Use the **Fill Tool** to drag the start and end path handles, or click on the object for a new start handle and drag out a new fill path. The gradient starts where you place the start handle, and ends where you place the end handle.

Each gradient fill type has a characteristic path. For example, Linear fills have single-line paths, while Radial fills have a two-line path so you can adjust the fill's extent in two directions away from the centre. If the object uses a **bitmap fill**, you'll see the fill path displayed as two lines joined at a centre point. Handles mark the fill's centre and edges.

Working with transparency

Transparency effects are great for highlights, shading and shadows, and simulating "rendered" realism. They can make the critical difference between flat-looking publications and publications with depth and snap. PagePlus fully supports variable transparency and lets you apply solid, gradient, or bitmap transparency to an object's fill or outline easily.

For example, in the illustration below, the butterflies have a solid (100% opaque) transparency, a gradient (100% to 0% opaque) transparency and a solid (50% opaque) transparency from left to right.

Transparencies work rather like fills that use "disappearing ink" instead of colour. The more transparency in a particular spot, the more "disappearing" takes place there, and the more the object(s) underneath show through. Just as a gradient fill can vary from light to dark, a transparency can vary from more to less, i.e. from clear to opaque, as in the illustration:

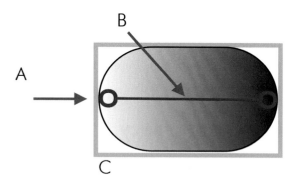

(A) Linear Transparency, (B) Path, (C) Effect on Object

Transparency types available in the Transparency tab are as follows:

- **Solid** transparency distributes the transparency uniformly.

- **Gradient** transparencies include linear, elliptical, and conical effects, ranging from clear to opaque.

- **Bitmap** transparencies include categorized texture maps based on the Swatches tab's selection of bitmaps.

Applying transparency

You can apply transparency to shapes, text frames, table cells, and to any artistic, frame, and table text.

To apply transparency with Transparency tab:

1. 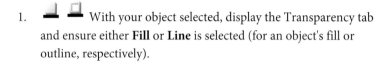 With your object selected, display the Transparency tab and ensure either **Fill** or **Line** is selected (for an object's fill or outline, respectively).

2. For solid transparency, select the ☐ **Solid** button and pick a thumbnail from the solid transparency gallery. The lighter thumbnails represent more transparency (expressed as percentage).
   - or -

   For gradient transparency, choose the 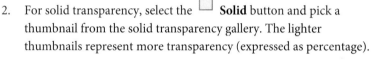 **Gradient** button and pick your thumbnail.
   - or -

   For bitmap transparency, choose the ⊞ ▾ **Bitmap** button and pick a thumbnail from a range of categories.

   The transparency is applied to the object's fill or outline.

3. Alternatively, drag the desired thumbnail from the gallery to an object, and release the mouse button.

To apply gradient transparency with the Transparency Tool:

1. Select the object and set the Transparency tab's Fill/Line swatch as before.

2.   Click the ⏺ **Transparency Tool** on the **Attributes** toolbar.

3.   Drag your cursor across the object and release the mouse button. The object takes a simple Linear transparency, grading from 100% opacity to 0% opacity (fully transparent).

Editing transparency

Once you've applied a gradient transparency, you can adjust or replace its **path** on the object, and the **level** of transparency along the path. You can even create more complex transparency effects by adding extra handles to the path by clicking and assigning different levels to each handle.

To adjust the transparency path:

•   Use the ⏺ **Transparency Tool** to drag individual handles, or click on the object for a new start handle and drag out a new transparency path. The effect starts where you place the start handle, and ends where you place the end handle. For bitmap transparencies, the path determines the centre and two edges of the effect.

Editing a **gradient transparency** path is similar to editing a comparable fill path. Adding a level of transparency means varying the transparency gradient by introducing a new **handle** and assigning it a particular value. For transparencies with multiple handles, each handle has its own value, comparable to a key colour in a gradient fill. Note that you cannot alter the values in a bitmap transparency.

To edit a gradient transparency directly:

1.   Select the object and set the Transparency tab's **Fill/Line** swatch as before.

2. Click the Q **Transparency Tool** on the **Attributes** toolbar. The
    object's transparency path appears on the fill or line, with start and
    end handles.

3. To **add** a transparency handle, drag from any **solid transparency**
    sample in the Transparency tab to the point on the path where you
    want to add the handle.

    The higher the percentage value assigned to a transparency handle,
    the more transparent the effect at that point.

4. To **change** the transparency value of any existing handle, including
    the start and end handles, select the handle and click on a new
    thumbnail in the Transparency tab's Solid transparency gallery (you
    can also drag your chosen thumbnail onto the selected handle).

5. To **move** a handle you've added, drag to a new position on the path.

6. To **delete** a handle you've added, select it and press the **Delete** key.

Understanding blend modes

You can think of **blend modes** as different rules for putting overlaying
pixels together to create a resulting colour. Note that blend modes work
in relation to the colours of the objects themselves (shapes, lines, and so
on).

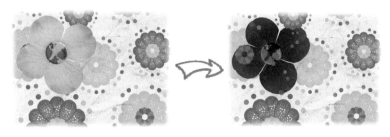

Yellow flower on page background

*The same flower with an **Exclusion** blend mode applied*

They are used for **creative effects** on overlapping objects, where colours blend on top of one another. Blend modes can be applied to both a top object's line and fill colour. You can adjust the blend mode of an existing object, or you can set the blend mode before creating a line, shape, etc.

For professional design, you can also make use of **composite blend modes**, or **isolated blending** within a group to prevent underlying objects from being affected by the blending operation.

To apply a blend mode to an existing object:

1.   Select an existing object on your page.

2.   On the **Colour** tab, choose from the **Blend Mode** drop-down list.

To apply a blend mode to a new line or shape:

1.   Select the line or shape tool you want to use, and set its appropriate settings—width, colour, etc.

2.   On the **Colour** tab, choose from the **Blend Mode** drop-down list.

3.   Create your line or shape on your page.

> Blend modes are also used when creating 2D and 3D effects.

For a complete list of blend modes, with supporting examples, please see the topic *Understanding blend modes* in PagePlus help.

Publishing and Sharing

10

Preflight check

Preflight is an essential process to ensure that your PagePlus output, whether PDF, HTML or eBook (both EPUB and EPUB 3 Fixed Layout), is published as intended. You can run a preflight check at any time during your design process to fix issues as they occur. In addition, when a problem is encountered on publishing, the preflight check will report the problem in the **Preflight** tab automatically, allowing you to check, locate, and fix the problem.

The example below shows elements of the page design which may generate warnings if publishing a document as a PDF.

*(**A**) Missing font style, (**B**) Low resolution image, (**C**) Unsupported form object, (**D**) Small hyperlink area, (**E**) Incompatible audio file*

It is not mandatory to resolve the warnings indicated in the Preflight check, in some cases PagePlus will work around the problem automatically on publication. However, by resolving the warnings, your final publication should provide users with a better experience when accessing your chosen output.

Manual preflight check

Checking your publication as you design is particularly useful when working toward a specific output which must comply with a rigid layout and style, such as HTML or eBook. You can then resolve problems as they arise, saving you time when you finally come to publish your publication.

To run a manual Preflight check:

1. Click **Preflight** at the bottom of your workspace to view the **Preflight** tab.

2. In the tab's drop-down list, select the desired publication type.

3. Click **Check** to run the preflight check.

   Any warnings will be listed in the **Preflight** tab.

> Some warnings may not be displayed during a manual preflight check as some problems are only specific to options chosen in the relevant Publish as dialogs.

To resolve problems listed in the Preflight check:

1. Select a warning from the list. A brief explanation of the warning displays at the bottom of the **Preflight** tab.

2. (Optional) Click **Help** to get immediate help on how to resolve your publishing problem.

3. Click **Locate** to automatically select the problem object.

4.   Modify the object as appropriate.

- or -

Click **Fix** to resolve the publishing problem automatically (not valid for all warnings).

5.   (Optional) Click **Check** to run the preflight check again.

This is useful once you've resolved a problem and you need to verify your fix before republishing.

Automated preflight check

PagePlus will automatically run a check of your document when you publish. This automated check is more comprehensive than the manual check discussed above as it also covers the options set in the Publish as dialogs. If there are any problems with the publication, the **Preflight** tab will automatically open, displaying a list of issues.

A warning dialog will also display, asking whether you wish to proceed with the export and ignore the listed problems. Click **Yes** to continue with publication or **No** to work through the issues before publishing.

To resolve the listed problems, follow the steps listed.

Interactive Print/PDF Preview

The **Print/PDF Preview** mode changes the screen view to display your page layout without frames, guides, rulers, and other screen items. Supporting toolbars allow for a comprehensive and interactive preview of your publication pages before printing or publishing as PDF.

*(**A**) Imposition toolbar, (**B**) Mail and Photo Merge toolbar (hidden by default), (**C**) Page Marks toolbar, (**D**) Margins toolbar, (**E**) Page Navigation tools, (**F**) Hintline toolbar, (**G**) View tools, (**H**) Printer toolbar, (**I**) Close toolbar, (**J**) View toolbar (hidden by default).*

The Preview is interactive—its main feature is to provide dynamic **print-time imposition**. Put simply, this allows you to create folded books, booklets, and more, **at the printing/publication stage** from unfolded basic publication setups. Other interactive features are also available while in Preview mode.

- Select installed printers, and choose which pages to print and how they print (to printer, file or separation).

- Add and adjust printer margins.

- Switch on/off page marks when generating professional output.

- Control which database records print when using mail and photo merge via a Mail and Photo Merge toolbar.

Don't forget to make the most of the Preview's powerful **viewing controls** hosted on the View toolbar. Use zoom controls, Pan/Zoom tools, and multi-page views for detailed preview work.

To preview the page:

1. Click **Print/PDF Preview** on the **Standard** toolbar.

    In Print/PDF Preview, your first printer sheet is displayed according to your printer's setup.

2. (Optional) Choose an installed printer from the **Printer** toolbar's drop-down list.

3. (Optional) Adjust printer margins from the **Margins** toolbar.

4. Review your publication using the page navigation controls at the bottom of your workspace.

To print via Printer toolbar:

1. Choose which page to print via the toolbar's **Print Publication** drop-down list.

2. Select **Print**.

The standard **Print** dialog is then displayed, where settings are carried over from Preview mode (see Printing basics on p. 150).

To publish as PDF via Printer toolbar:

•   Select **Publish PDF**.

The standard **Publish PDF** dialog is then displayed (see Publishing PDF files on p. 153).

To cancel Preview mode:

•   Select **Close Preview** from the top of your workspace (or click the window's **Close** button).

Document imposition in Preview mode

During preview, you can enable imposition of your document, choosing a mode suited to your intended final publication (book, booklet, etc.). Each mode displays different toolbar options on the context-sensitive **Imposition** toolbar. Document imposition is not limited to desktop printing—it can also be used when creating a press-ready PDF for professional printing.

To choose an imposition mode:

- From the **Imposition** toolbar, select an option from the **Imposition Mode** drop-down list.

Printing books and booklets

To produce double-sided sheets, click **Print** and use the Print dialog's Double-sided Printing or Manual Duplex options (under More Options). Ensure your printer is setup for double-sided printing or run sheets through twice, printing first the front and then the back of the sheet (reverse top and bottom between runs). The sheets can then be collated and bound at their centre to produce a booklet, with all the pages in the correct sequence.

Printing basics

Printing your publication to a desktop printer is one of the more likely operations you'll be performing in PagePlus. The easy-to-use Print dialog presents the most commonly used options to you, with a navigable "live" Preview window to check your print output.

The dialog also supports additional printing options via the **More Options** button including **Double-sided Printing**, **Mail Merge**,

Rasterize, and many other useful printing options. One particular option, called **Layout**, allows for print-time imposition of your publication—simply create a booklet or other folded publication at the print stage.

Here we'll cover what you need to know for basic desktop printer output. If you're working with a service bureau or professional printer and need to provide PDF output, see Publishing PDF files (p. 153).

To set up your printer or begin printing:

1. (Optional) To print selected text or objects, make your selection on the page.

2. Click 🖶 **Print** on the **Standard** toolbar. The **Print** dialog appears.

To set your printing options:

1. Select a currently installed printer from the **Printer** drop-down list. If necessary, click the **Properties** button to set up the printer for the correct page size, etc.

2. Select a printer profile from the **Profile** drop-down list. You can just use **Current Settings** or choose a previously saved custom profile (.ppr) based on a combination of dialog settings; **Browse** lets you navigate to any .ppr file on your computer. To save current settings, click the **Save As** button, and provide a unique profile name. The profile is added to the drop-down list.

    > 💡 If you modify any profile settings, an asterisk appears next to the profile name.

3. Select the number of copies to print, and optionally instruct the printer to **Collate** them.

4. Select the print **Range** to be printed, e.g. the Entire Publication, Current Page, Current Selection (if selected text or objects in step 1), or range of pages. For specific pages or a range of pages, enter

"1,3,5" or "2-5", or enter any combination of the two.

Whichever option you've chosen, the **Include** drop-down list lets you export all sheets in the range, or just odd or even sheets, with the option of printing in **Reverse** order.

5. Set a percentage **Scale** which will enlarge or shrink your print output (both page and contents). A 100% scale factor creates a full size print output. Alternatively, from the adjacent drop-down list, choose **Shrink to Fit** to reduce your publication's page size to the printer sheet size or **Scale to Fit** to enlarge or reduce the publication page size as required.

6. Keep **Auto Rotate** checked if you want your publication page to automatically rotate your printer's currently set sheet orientation. When you access the Print dialog, if page and sheet sizes do not match, you'll be prompted to adjust your printer sheet orientation automatically (or you can just ignore auto-rotation).

7. Select an option from the **Work around printer problems** drop-down list. **Best Quality** is selected by default, but occasionally problems arise with some printer drivers when bitmaps in a publication use transparency. If you are getting poor results, you can select the **Send As Bitmap** option to output whole pages as bitmaps. While slower, this approach virtually guarantees successful printing.

8. Click **Print**.

Trimmed Mode

Trimmed Mode is similar to Print/PDF Preview, letting you view your page exactly how it will appear in print. Visible guides, objects partly on the pasteboard, text marks, and special characters will all be hidden so your preview is realistic.

To enter trimmed mode:

- From the **View** menu, click **Trimmed Mode**.

You can select the option again to exit Trimmed Mode.

> Objects are cropped by the page boundaries, not the print boundaries.
>
> You can still edit page content while Trimmed Mode is enabled.

More print options

Additional print options are available from the Print dialog if you're planning to use imposition at print time (see p. 150), use specific PagePlus features which use printing (e.g., Mail Merge), print double-sided, or generate professional output.

Publishing PDF files

PagePlus can output your publications to PDF (Portable Document Format), a cross-platform WYSIWYG file format developed by Adobe, intended to handle documents in a device- and platform-independent manner.

PDF documents are ideal for both **web-ready** distribution and **professional** printing.

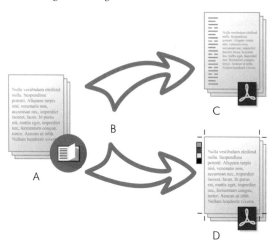

*(**A**) PagePlus Publication, (**B**) Preflight and Publish, (**C**) web-ready PDF, (**D**) Press-ready PDF (professional).*

In PagePlus, ready-to-go PDF profiles are available for both uses, making PDF setup less complicated.

Preflight checking

To assist you as you design, you can perform a manual preflight check as you go. On publishing, a preflight check is also run automatically, alerting you to any design problems that would result in sub-optimal published results. See Preflight check on p. 145 for more information.

The preflight check also offers solutions to resolve PDF publishing issues.

Publishing to PDF

To publish as a PDF file (using a profile):

1. Click ⬛ **Publish as PDF** on the **Standard** toolbar.

2. Select a profile for screen-ready or professional output from the **Profile** drop-down list.

   The dialog updates with the selected profile's new settings. The **Compatibility** is set according to the profile and doesn't need to be changed.

3. Select the **Range** to be published, e.g. the Entire Publication, Current Page, or range of pages. For specific pages or a range of pages, enter "1,3,5" or "2-5", or enter any combination of the two .

4. Set a percentage **Scale** which will enlarge or shrink your published output (both page and contents). A 100% scale factor creates a full size print output.

5. Click ⬇ **More Options** and make additional settings as required including **Layout**, **Prepress**, and **Colour Management**.

6. Click **Publish**.

Saving PDF profiles

To save any current combination of your own PDF output settings as a custom publish profile with a unique name, click the **Save As** button next to the Publish profile list. In a subsequent session you can recall the profile by selecting its name from the list.

Publishing as eBooks

The emergence of eBooks in recent years offers not just the traditional book publishers an opportunity to explore new electronic book markets, but also provides the writer with the ability to directly publish their own eBooks, and for fully designed layouts to be published for eBook readers.

In PagePlus, you can be your own publisher and create flowing eBooks in both EPUB and Kindle mobi formats, and fixed-layout eBooks in EPUB 3 format. Like publishing to PDF and HTML, the process of eBook publishing is straightforward, with the added benefit of manual and automatic preflight checking to ensure your file conforms to eBook standards.

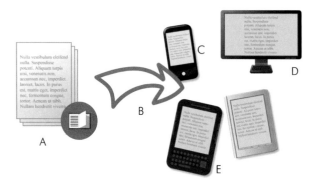

(A) *PagePlus Publication,* *(B)* *Preflight and Publish,* *(C)* *Smart phone,* *(D)* *Computer,* *(E)* *Kindle/EPUB readers.*

Preflight checking

To assist you as you design, you can perform a manual preflight check as you go. On publishing, a preflight check is also run automatically, alerting you to any design problems that would result in sub-optimal published results. See Preflight check on p. 145 for more information.

The preflight check also offers solutions to resolve EPUB 2 and EPUB 3 publishing warnings (see PagePlus Help).

Publishing

Different approaches can be taken depending on whether you are publishing flowing or fixed-layout eBooks, and which file format you wish to publish, i.e. EPUB or Kindle mobi. Kindle publishing additionally requires the KindleGen program to be installed.

To publish a flowing or fixed layout eBook:

1. Choose **Publish As**> from the **File** menu and select **eBook** from the submenu.

2. With the Output menu item selected, from the **Profile** drop-down menu select a flowing or fixed option according to the type of device you want to publish to. Alternatively, ignore profiles to fully customize settings yourself.

3. From the dialog's Document Info>Metadata menu, add metadata and an ID (if needed).

4. With the Document Info>Cover menu item selected, for a pre-designed eBook cover, either enter a path to a picture in the **Use File** field or click **Use Page** and choose a page from your publication. You can create cover art in PagePlus, PhotoPlus or DrawPlus).

5. Click **Publish**.

6. In the **Publish eBook** dialog, navigate to the location where you wish to publish your eBook, then enter a file name in the **File name** box. Keep the **Save as type** drop-down list set to "EPUB files (*.epub)" or "Kindle files (*.mobi)" as appropriate.

7. Click **Save**.

To publish an eBook for Kindle:

1. Install the KindleGen program (download from Amazon Kindle publishing).

2. Follow the procedure for publishing flowing or fixed-layout eBooks above, choosing a Kindle publishing profile.

3. In the Publish as eBook dialog's Kindle section, click **Browse** to navigate to (and select) the kindlegen.exe file from the installed folder above and click **Publish**.

4. Navigate to a folder, choose a filename for your eBook, and change the **Save as type** drop-down list to "Kindle files (*.mobi)".

5. Click **Save**.

If you checked **Preview eBook file**, in the Output section of the Publish as eBook dialog, the file will open in its associated reader if one is installed.

Once you've published your eBook you'll want to make it available to a physical device as soon as possible. Typical ways that your eBook can be read include:

- Via computer: Install standalone software such as Azardi or use a Google Chrome plug-in such as Readium to view your EPUB document. Similarly, Kindle Previewer software is the choice for Kindle files.

- Via Kindle: Transfer your published *.mobi file by copying to your device via your USB port. Alternatively, you can send your file via email directly to your device.

- Via EPUB device/Smart phone: Like Kindle devices, you can transfer your *.epub file to your device via USB.

Additional Information

11

Contacting Serif

Help with your Product

   community.serif.com
Get answers and ask questions in
the Serif community!

Additional Serif information

Serif website   www.serif.com

Main office	
Address	The Software Centre, PO Box 2000 Nottingham, NG11 7GW, UK
Phone	(0115) 914 2000
Phone (Registration)	(0800) 376 1989 +44 800 376 1989 800-794-6876 (US, Canada)
Phone (Sales)	(0800) 376 7070 +44 800 376 7070 800-489-6703 (US, Canada)
Customer Service	0845 345 6770 800-489-6720 (US, Canada)
Fax	(0115) 914 2020

Credits

This User Guide, and the software described in it, is furnished under an end user License Agreement, which is included with the product. The agreement specifies the permitted and prohibited uses.

Trademarks

Serif is a registered trademark of Serif (Europe) Ltd.

PagePlus is a registered trademark of Serif (Europe) Ltd.

All Serif product names are trademarks of Serif (Europe) Ltd.

Microsoft, Windows, and the Windows logo are registered trademarks of Microsoft Corporation. All other trademarks acknowledged.

Windows Vista and the Windows Vista Start button are trademarks or registered trademarks of Microsoft Corporation in the United States and/or other countries.

Kindle, the AmazonKindle logo, and Whispersync are trademarks of Amazon.com, Inc. or its affiliates.

Nook is a trademark of Barnes & Noble, Inc.

Copyrights

Digital Images ©2008 Hemera Technologies Inc. All Rights Reserved.

Bitstream Font content © 1981-2005 Bitstream Inc. All rights reserved.

Portions images © 1997-2002 Nova Development Corporation; © 1995 Expressions Computer Software; © 1996-98 CreatiCom, In.; 1996 Cliptoart; © 1997 Multimedia Agency Corporation; © 1997-98 Seattle Support Group. Rights of all parties reserved.

This application was developed using LEADTOOLS, copyright © 1991-2007 LEAD Technologies, Inc. ALL Rights Reserved.

Panose Typeface Matching System ©1991, 1992, 1995-97 Hewlett-Packard Corporation.

THE PROXIMITY HYPHENATION SYSTEM © 1989 Proximity Technology Inc. All rights reserved.

THE PROXIMITY/COLLINS DATABASE © 1990 William Collins Sons & Co. Ltd.; © 1990 Proximity Technology Inc. All rights reserved.

THE PROXIMITY/MERRIAM-WEBSTER DATABASE® © 1990 Merriam-Webster Inc.; © 1990 Proximity Technology Inc. All rights reserved.

The Sentry Spelling-Checker Engine © 2000 Wintertree Software Inc.

The ThesDB Thesaurus Engine © 1993-97 Wintertree Software Inc.

WGrammar Grammar-Checker Engine © 1998 Wintertree Software Inc.

Extensible Metadata Platform (XMP) Copyright © 2006 Adobe Systems Incorporated. All rights reserved.

ICC Colour Profiles © 2006 Adobe Systems Incorporated. All rights reserved.

PANTONE® Colours displayed in the software application or in the user documentation may not match PANTONE-identified standards. Consult current PANTONE Colour Publications for accurate colour. PANTONE® and other Pantone trademarks are the property of Pantone LLC. ©Pantone LLC, 2014.

Pantone LLC is the copyright owner of colour data and/or software which are licensed to Serif (Europe) Ltd. to distribute for use only in combination with PagePlus. PANTONE Colour Data and/or Software shall not be copied onto another disk or into memory unless as part of the execution of PagePlus.

FontForge © 2000,2001,2002,2003,2004,2005,2006,2007,2008 by George Williams.

Portions of this software are copyright © 2008 The FreeType Project (www.freetype.org). All rights reserved.

ODF Translator © 2006-2008, Clever Age, DIaLOGIKa, Sonata Software Ltd. All rights reserved.

Office Binary Translator to OpenXML Copyright © 2008-2009, DIaLOGIKa. All rights reserved.

Anti-Grain Geometry - Version 2.4 Copyright © 2002-2005 Maxim Shemanarev (McSeem)

Clipart samples from Serif ArtPacks © Serif (Europe) Ltd. & Paul Harris

TrueType font samples from Serif FontPacks © Serif (Europe) Ltd.

Companies and names used in samples are fictitious.

Index